£6.95

CW01661011

M

QA

Questions & Answers

Fundamentals of Marketing

MARKETING

Q&A

Questions & Answers

Fundamentals of Marketing

Peter Doust

Financial Training

First published in Great Britain 1986 by Financial Training Publications Limited, Avenue House, 131 Holland Park Avenue, London W11 4UT

ISBN: 1 85185 000 7

Typeset and produced by Graham Burn, Leighton Buzzard, Beds.
Printed by Pendragon Press, Cambridge

Contents

Contents

Introduction

All of the questions and answers contained in this book have been specificially written for students who are taking the Fundamentals of Marketing examination paper for the Certificate I stage of the Institute of Marketing examinations.

This book contains 80 questions and answers and is arranged in eight chapters which cover all aspects of the Institute of Marketing syllabus. The breakdown is as follows:

1. Origins, developments and concepts of marketing
2. Distribution
3. The scope and value of marketing research
4. The organisation of marketing
5. Product planning
6. Pricing
7. Selling
8. Advertising and sales promotion

At the beginning of each section, readers will find an expanded breakdown of each section showing the exact syllabus requirements of the Institute of Marketing.

Although the questions follow the Institute of Marketing syllabus they will also be found useful by students of marketing on such courses as: HND in business studies; BA in business studies; Organisation and Marketing Management for the ICMA; as well as offering a wide coverage for any student being introduced to the subject on short courses.

Students will find these questions and answers particularly useful if used in conjunction with the textbooks recommended by the Institute of Marketing.

It should be remembered that the aim of the Fundamentals of Marketing paper is to ensure that students gain an understanding and appreciation of the basic concepts and philosophies of marketing, as well as an understanding of marketing terminology.

Regardless of what method of study a student has used, these questions and answers will provide an essential tool which, if properly used, will assist in a greater understanding of the course, with an improved chance of success in the examination.

We suggest that the greatest benefit will be shown if students follow this procedure: firstly, thoroughly read each question, breaking it down into its component parts; secondly, establish the theory or theories that are required in fully covering all aspects of the question; thirdly, establish a skeleton answer, giving just headings and subheadings. Finally, when writing your full answer, give real-life examples whenever possible.

Students should also be reminded that the Fundamentals of Marketing paper offers a very wide choice of questions that cover all of the basic concepts and precepts of marketing. In this examination, the Institute designs questions in such a way that candidates who demonstrate an understanding of these basic concepts and precepts should do well in the examination.

Additionally, the Institute encourages students, that wherever possible, to give practical examples in order to demonstrate a good understanding of these theories and the ability to apply them in the real world.

If a student thinks creatively, or originally, about a particular situation, as opposed to just relying upon a textbook answer, he is more likely to gain high marks.

Always remember that answers to questions *must* cover the specific question, and that questions *only*, in a clear, concise manner.

The Institute of Marketing indicate that many students fail to get good marks in this examination by using poor examination techniques. Some of the reasons they have given are: a failure to understand the question, and therefore, a failure to answer it; wasting too much time by writing too much on one question; poor presentation; and a poor selection of questions answered.

The Institute suggests that these weaknesses could probably be overcome if students took the following advice:

Ensure that you understand the question, and if in any doubt, tackle another one;

be sure that when the question asks for illustrations, or when it requests an answer in report form, that you do this;

always resist the rather natural temptation in an examination, to write everything that is known about a general subject instead of limiting your answer to the specific area asked in the question;

as mentioned earlier, the Institute suggests that you sketch out a framework for answers before beginning to write;

and finally, they suggest that you should *not* adhere strictly to textbook answers, and that you should illustrate your answers from your own experience wherever this is possible.

Try and remember that marketing is a subject that many people think they know a lot about.

As consumers, all of us are active participants in the marketing system. Many hold the opinion that 'marketing is just common sense'. We know that when an advertisement fails to please us, it is ineffective. A shop should not be out of the product that we want.

'Wholesalers are unnecessary' and 'the seller who sells direct can sell for less money', 'if products are offered at lower prices in nicer shops and with more liberal credit terms, many more units can be sold'. This is all 'common sense' to many consumers, and if it is not, they possess an 'uncommon' sense of marketing. The truth about these statements is that the offending advertisements may make consumers remember the product and its benefits, which may be one of the reasons they buy the product; or the advertisement may not suit them, but it may be effective on truly prospective customers. No shop tries to stock all the goods that may be wanted by all customers. Instead most stores try to serve a segment of the market in a manner that will encourage customer-loyalty. 'Buy direct and save' is a typical appeal to common sense, but unfortunately the direct seller normally has higher market costs than the distribution channel employing the wholesaler. To cap the common sense discussion, the price can be too low as well as too high, and credit terms and other services are often too liberal, rather than too conservative.

The moral of these examples is that your common sense and intuition about marketing should not be trusted until you have a thorough understanding of the marketing system. The Fundamentals of Marketing Course is designed to give you just that.

Good luck in your studies.

1 Origins, developments and concepts of marketing

INTRODUCTION

This chapter contains questions and answers designed to cover the origins and development of the marketing concept; the importance of satisfying customer needs; the structure of markets; the functions of marketing; the impact of external environmental factors on marketing operations; consumerism and the elements of the marketing mix.

QUESTIONS

1 'It is possible to define marketing under two different groupings, the "classical" and the "modern".' Discuss.

2 What do you understand by the marketing concept?

3 Explain the basic differences between the philosophies of selling and marketing.

4 What are the basic functions of marketing?

5 What do you understand by the term 'marketing environment'?

6 In any marketing operation, there are numerous factors over which the company has no control. One vital factor is its consumers. Why is this and how can a company overcome this problem?

7 Describe the development of the marketing concept.

8 What constitutes the macromarketing system?

9 What responsibilities does marketing management have towards its customers?

10 Describe, with the use of charts, the main forms of marketing organisation.

ANSWERS

1 It is possible to define marketing under two categories: the 'classical' which refers to a narrow category; and the 'modern', which is much broader.

Applying the classical definition, marketing can be defined as 'the performance of business activities that direct the flow of goods and services from producer to consumer or user', or 'the process that a society adopts by which the demand structure for economic goods and services is anticipated or enlarged and satisfied through the promotion, physical distribution, and conception of goods and services'.

Both of these classical definitions direct themselves towards the physical movement of economic goods and services, and in so doing display several weaknesses. They tend, for example, to overvalue the roles of marketing channels and physical distribution. Both government and non-profit institutions are completely ignored when, in this modern day, they are extremely important. The importance of exchange between buyers and sellers — such as unions, groups of consumers, government departments, shareholders, employees — is again not considered.

A more up-to-date definition of marketing which shows a broader approach, must not confine itself to economic goods and services. It should cover organisations such as charities, the St. John's Ambulance Brigade; people such as film stars, pop stars and politicians; places, particularly holiday resorts; and also ideas, showing the public or social responsibility to its market. The significant factor is that the most important person in any definition of marketing must be the consumer. A company can only achieve its objectives by satisfying its customers, and marketing is not just concerned with enlarging demand. It must also attempt to match supply with demand. The social and public responsibility of marketing (marketing ethics, product safety) must also be included, as well as the question of whether a product *should* be sold, not only whether it *can* be sold.

In the context of what has just been said, a broader, modern definition of marketing would be: 'Marketing is the anticipation, management and satisfaction of demand through the exchange process.' Marketing involves places, people, ideas, organisations and services, as well as products.

If companies are going to forecast adequately the demand for a product, they must carry out consumer research on a regular basis, as well as managing demand. The activities of marketing can be directed to consumers and to publics; consumer demand refers to the characteristics and needs of the final consumer, the industrial consumers, wholesalers, retailers and supermarkets, government departments, international markets and non-profit organisations. A firm can appeal to one of these or a combination of them. Nevertheless, the process of marketing is incomplete until consumers and publics exchange their money, or their promise to pay, or their support, for the offering of the firm, person, place, or idea.

In conclusion one can therefore state that marketing involves anticipation, requiring the firm to conduct research; management which involves stimulating, facilitating, and regulating demand; and satisfaction for filling expectations. Also, demand is affected by the characteristics and needs of both consumers and publics. Finally, exchange completes the process.

2 The marketing concept is a consumer-oriented, integrated, goal-oriented philosophy for a firm, institution or person. Figure 1 should help to illustrate this concept.

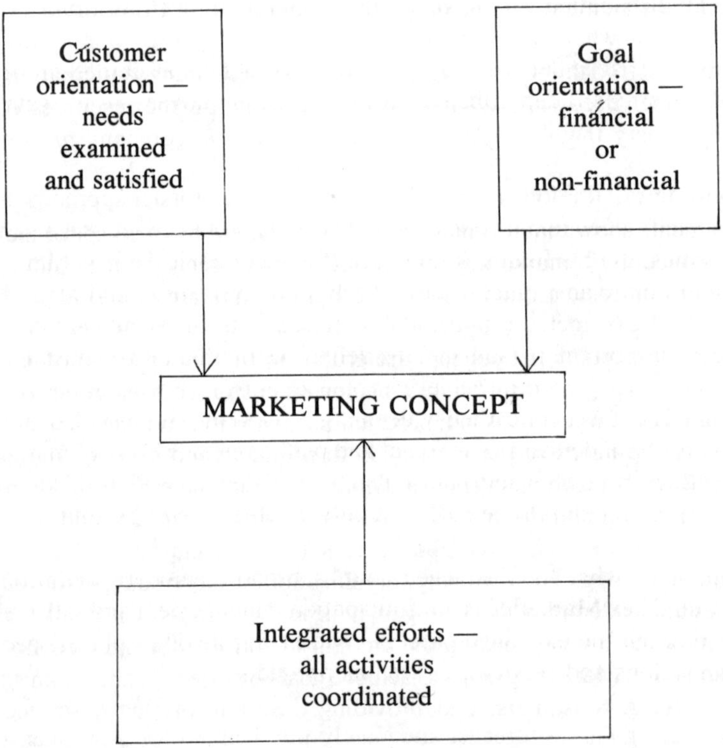

Figure 1

One of the best known authorities on management and marketing, Peter Drucker, emphasised the role of marketing in the success of the business. What he said in 1954 is just as valid today:

> If we want to know what a business is, we must start with its purpose . . . There is only one valid definition of business purpose: to create a customer. What business thinks it produces is not of first importance, especially not to the future of the business, or to its success. What the customer thinks he is buying, what he considers 'value' is decisive, it determines what a business is, what it produces, and whether it will prosper.

Over the past two or three decades, many organisations have established their own definitions, and reliance upon marketing. A few examples might help to illustrate this approach.

'Instead of trying to market what is easiest for us to make, we must find out much more about what the consumer is willing to buy. In other words, we must apply our creativeness more intelligently to people and their needs, rather than to products'. This statement was made by the General Food Corporation.

B.G. Goodrich stated that marketing is 'the process of defining, anticipating, and creating customer needs and wants and of organising all the resources of the company to satisfy them at a greater total profit to the company *and* to the customer'.

These statements show that for many companies, the era has arrived for them to apply the concept of marketing; marketing is now seen as the underlying philosophy of business, around which all other pursuits are made.

The different elements of the concept are crucial to the final success of either a product, a service, an organisation, or a person. A customer orientation requires an examination of market needs, not production capability, and development of a plan to satisfy the needs of the market. Both products and services should be viewed as means to accomplish ends and not be the end in themselves. Under an integrated marketing philosophy, all activities relating to services and products are coordinated, including finances, production, research and development, stock control, and marketing. The company, organisation or individual person should be goal-oriented and employ marketing to achieve these goals. The goals may be profit, curing a disease, increasing the amount of tourism, or the election of a political candidate. Marketing helps to achieve goals by orienting the organisation towards satisfying consumers, and providing desirable products, services or ideas.

The concept is nevertheless only a guide to planning. The company must also consider its strengths and weaknesses in its different functional areas. Marketing plans need to balance the goals of the company, the needs of their customers, and the capability of the resources available to them. Additionally, the impact of competition, government rules and regulations, and the other external environmental factors must also be evaluated.

3 Figure 2 illustrates the differences between the two philosophies of selling and marketing. The benefits from marketing, as opposed to sales, are numerous. The marketing philosophy concentrates on the analysis of consumers and satisfying those consumers, as well as directing all of the resources of the company to make both the products and services that their customers want; it has sufficient flexibility to adapt not only to changes in the needs of consumers, but also to changes in consumers themselves. With a marketing philosophy, selling is but one tool used to communicate with, and to understand, customers; consumer dissatisfaction fed back through the salesforce, can lead to changes in company policy, not just a different sales approach. Marketing genuinely looks for the real differences in the tastes of consumers, and develops products and services to satisfy those tastes. It is oriented to the long term, and the goals of marketing should reflect the overall goals of the company. Marketing views the needs of customers in a very broad way, rather than a narrow way.

Despite the obvious advantages of this approach, and although many marketing departments acknowledge the importance of marketing, in fact only a few of them really understand and practice marketing in its truest sense.

The chief executive of the Ford Motor Company once said:

> I thought we were doing marketing. We have a group marketing director, a skilled advertising department, and elaborate market-planning procedures. These fooled us. When the crunch came, I realised that we weren't producing the cars the people wanted. We weren't responding to new needs. Our marketing operation was nothing more than a glorified sales department.

4 The basic functions of marketing are:

(a) *Environmental analysis and marketing research* This consists of monitoring the external factors affecting the success or failure of the firm (such as the economy and competition), and the collection of data to resolve specific marketing issues.

(b) *Consumer analysis* The examination and evaluation of consumer characteristics, needs and purchase processes.

(c) *Product (service) planning* The development and maintenance of products, product assortments, product positions, brands, packaging, and deletion of old products.

(d) *Distribution planning* This is the establishment of distribution channel relations, physical distribution, the management of inventory, warehousing, transportation, the allocation of goods, wholesaling and retailing.

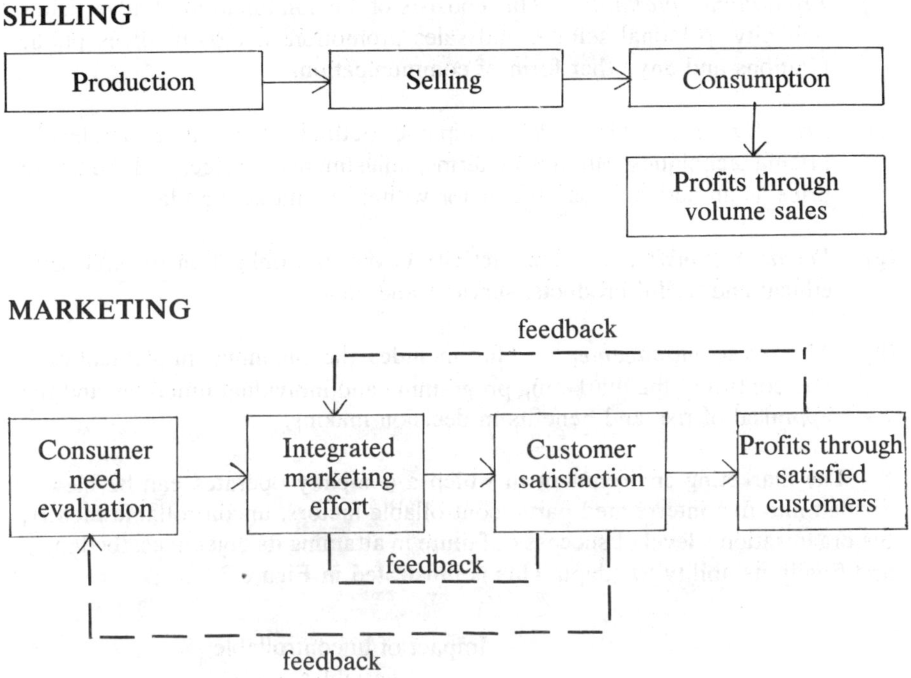

Marketing philosophy	Sales philosophy
● consumer-oriented	● sales-oriented
● two-way process (interactive)	● one-way process
● appropriate adaptation to environment	● little adaptation to environment
● broad view of consumer needs	● narrow view of consumer needs
● emphasis on groups of consumers	● emphasis on single customers
● marketing research determines output	● output 'sold' to consumers
● long-run goals	● short-run goals
● profit-oriented	● volume-oriented
● integrated planning and feedback	● informal planning and feedback

Figure 2

(e) *Promotional planning* This consists of the combination of advertising, publicity, personal selling, and sales promotion; it also involves public relations and any other form of communication.

(f) *Price planning* This task encompasses outlining price ranges and levels, pricing techniques, purchasing terms, adjustments to price, and the use of price as an active or passive factor within the marketing plan.

(g) *Social responsibility* This activity covers the obligation to offer safe, ethical and useful products, services and ideas.

(h) *Marketing management* This includes the planning, implementation and control of the marketing programme and individual functions and the appraisal of risk and benefits in decision-making.

5 The marketing environment in which a company operates can be clearly divided into five interrelated parts: controllable factors, uncontrollable factors, the organisation's level of success or failure in attaining its objectives, feedback, and finally its ability to adapt. This is illustrated in Figure 3.

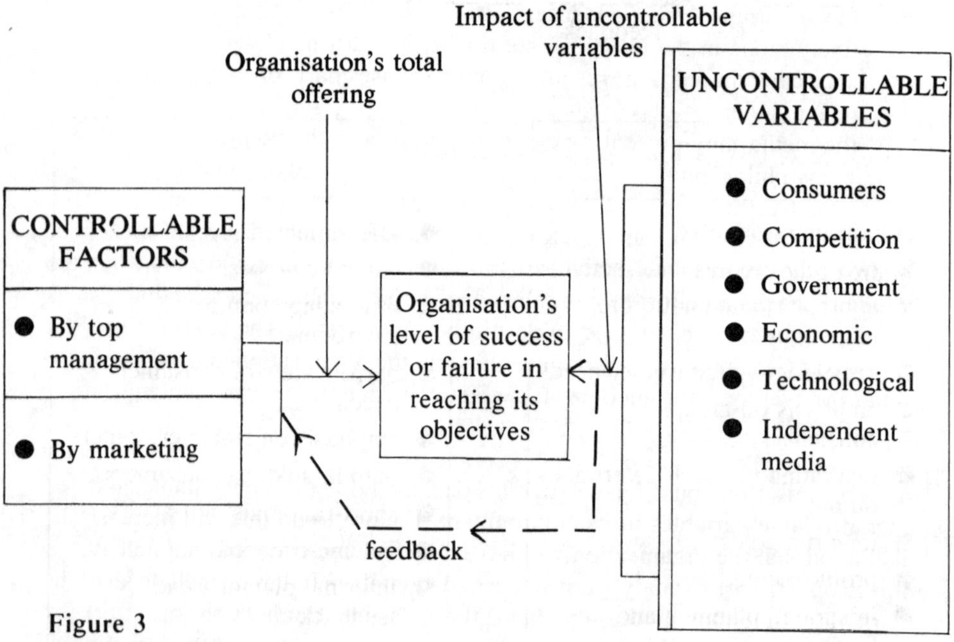

Figure 3

Firstly, the controllable factors are those factors that are directed by the company and the marketing department. Also, a number of basic interrelated decisions are, of course, made by the senior management and the board of directors of the company. Such decisions include the choice of the type of business that the company is to be involved in, the corporate or strategic objectives that the company will adopt, the role that marketing will play, and the role of the other functions of the organisation as a whole. Then, and only then, marketing management make a number of decisions based upon the outcome of the foregoing activities. Such decisions must contain the selection and clear segmentation of the market, the setting of clearly defined marketing objectives, establishing the organisational structure for marketing less suited to the marketing objectives, setting up the marketing plans, and finally confirming the necessary control techniques in order to command the whole operation effectively. If all of these factors are combined, this results in the ability to establish an overall marketing strategy for the company.

The major factors outside the control of the company are: its customers, the state of competition, government intervention, economic factors, technological change, and the various independent media that operate in the environment. All of these have an impact on how well the marketing organisation and the company as a whole are accepted. Many factors can interfere with this, for example:

(a) competition may lower prices;
(b) because of different cultural beliefs, a product may not be popular with one segment of the market;
(c) the government may enact legislation;
(d) fluctuations in the inflation rate might slow down sales;
(e) shortages in certain resources may cause part of a product to be unavailable;
(f) the media may present a negative image about the company.

Consequently, the offering of the company and the impact on the company of the uncontrollable environmental factors interact to determine the level of success or failure of the organisation in achieving its objectives. Feedback occurs when the company makes an effort to monitor these uncontrollable factors and assess its own strengths and weaknesses, opportunities and threats. The adaption process refers to any changes in its marketing plan that the organisation makes in order to bypass or overcome the uncontrollable factors within the environment in which it is operating.

Any organisation must be willing to consider both the controllable and the uncontrollable variables in its environment. Failure to do this will increase the likelihood that the organisation will have a lack of direction and not achieve its objectives. Failure to analyse consumers adequately, a failure to include all of the marketing functions necessary, and the possible duplication of effort by interdepartmental rivalry may lead to missed opportunities and the retention of undesirable products or services. The company may find it impossible to deal with certain channels in the distribution area, and it may well have disputes with different channels within distribution. Entirely the wrong image might be generated by an inefficient balance within the marketing mix, or ineffective promotion.

Unless an organisation is prepared to carry out an adequate analysis of the environment, the whole organisation may also violate social norms and values. In consequence, it may well not maintain a competitive edge over its competitors. There is also considerable danger in the company violating new laws with the consequence that the number of consumer complaints increases. Also, changes in the unemployment situation and in inflation can incur bad reactions to the company, as will failures to use new technology in producing better products. If the environment is not regularly monitored and the company does not adapt to the environmental changes, this may result in the organisation's lack of overall direction with the consequent poor results.

6 The uncontrollable factors are those elements that affect an organisation's performance and that cannot be directly controlled by either the organisation or the marketing department. These are extremely important and a failure to consider them often results in a failure of the marketing plan. They must, therefore, be continually monitored and any changes in these factors must be incorporated into an updated marketing plan.

As the whole concept and philosophy of marketing surrounds consumers and customers, and as this is a vital uncontrollable variable, it must receive a high level of attention from marketers.

Although marketers have control over various aspects of the target market, they do not control the different and varying characteristics of the population that make up that target market. Companies can react to, but not control, the different characteristics of consumers, such as: income, occupation, age, marital status, education, race, geographical location, and type of living accommodation. One of the best examples that one can use is baby foods. Whereas a company can develop baby foods, it has no control over the declining number of births. Therefore, if a baby-food company is to continue to grow, it must expand into other products and services. Marketing management must understand the interpersonal implications of consumer behaviour. Any products or services that consumers purchase are affected by such factors as family, religion, education, custom, friends, standards of performance, as well as the factors that shape the cultures, subcultures and society as a whole. At present, for example, in many parts of England, shops are not allowed to open on a Sunday, and if they are allowed to open, are restricted as to the type of goods that can be sold. The sale of alcoholic beverages is strictly controlled, not only as to price, but also as to when they can be sold, who can buy them and when shops can open. Cinemas and the films that they show are very closely rated. In Scotland, however, many of these factors do not apply as the rules in Scotland are considerably different to those in England.

One must also consider that because consumers act differently in purchasing the various types of products and services, marketing personnel need to understand the consumer-decision process. This process explains the steps through which a consumer passes when buying a product. For example, to purchase a motor car, the consumer very carefully searches for information about a number of different motor cars, will shortlist and rank several alternatives, select a favourite, negotiate a financial deal, and then finally complete the purchase. On the other hand, with a hamburger, the consumer looks at how much time he has, and goes to the nearest McDonald's or Wimpy so that he can have his lunch in the time that is allocated.

In the mid-1980s consumer groups and consumer organisations speak out very strongly on behalf of consumers, particularly in front of the media. If marketing organisations are to avoid negative consequences brought about by very active levels of consumerism, they must communicate with the consumers, they must anticipate problems, as well as responding to complaints, thus ensuring that the company operates properly.

7 Between 1950 and 1960 many companies progressed from a sales orientation to a marketing orientation. This was particularly obvious in the market for consumer durables. Many companies found during that decade that the supply they had of consumer durables exceeded the demand in the face of the purchasing power of consumers. This was probably the first time that a true buyers' market was experienced; consumers had the money, but they were not buying the products.

Even so, many marketers still continued to be oriented towards the sales concept; they still tried to push the existing products, they increased their selling efforts, they repeated the same themes in selling, and they still tried to unload excessively large inventories of stock. However, some marketers had greater foresight, and recognised the need, since consumers' requirements were unending, to develop a greater diversity of products to meet these needs. It was no longer acceptable to make minor alterations to existing products.

One of the best examples to quote is the General Electric Company. In the 1950s, GEC stated that:

> The principal task of the marketing function is not so much to be skilful in making the customer do what suits the interest of the business, as to be skilful in conceiving and then making the business do what suits the interests of the customer. The marketing concepts integrate marketing into each phase of the business. Thus, marketing through its studies and research, will establish for the engineer, the design and manufacturing person, what the customer wants in a given product, what price he or she is willing to pay, and where and when it will be wanted.

Many of the marketing activities have changed as a result of the development of the marketing concept:

(a) *A greater emphasis on new product development* This results in a greater diversity of products which are required to meet the needs of customers.

(b) *A much heavier emphasis on market segmentation* Consumers with similar needs were identified, and strategies were directed to these particular segments.

(c) *More intense focusing on marketing communications* It was now vital that the benefits of products had to be communicated to the different segments of consumers. In a sales orientation there was a tendency for advertising to be repetitive and simple, but under the marketing concept, advertising was considerably more diverse and therefore more likely to inform consumers about product benefits.

(d) *A more positive and creative approach in personal selling* Salemen firstly had to determine the needs of their customers and then develop their sales approach accordingly. No longer could they afford a standardised approach to selling.

(e) *The creation of more selective media and distributive outlets* There are now considerably more specialised magazines, a greater use of direct mail, and more speciality wholesalers and retailers.

(f) *Encouraging marketing research* The information requirements on consumer needs became urgent. More and more frequent use was made of consumer surveys to identify opportunities, as well as new products undergoing more rigorous consumer testing.

These changes did not occur quickly. Even companies such as the General Electric Company who were quick to recognise the changes, were still the exception to the rule. Even today, some companies are still operating on the basis of a production orientation or a sales orientation.

8 The broad macromarketing system is made up of the environmental forces that shape demand as well as influencing the resources that are available to the company. Therefore, in developing marketing plans, marketing management must consider these forces. Firstly, at the very centre of the macromarketing system is the consumer, this being the central issue of the marketing philosophy. Secondly, there is an element made up of the different components of marketing strategy. These, of course, are directly within the control of the company. Thirdly, there is the element in the total marketing system made up of the facilitating organisations. These are organisations that are required to implement marketing strategy, such as wholesalers, retailers in respect of the distribution functions, advertising agencies, various media agencies for effective communications, and marketing research companies to provide marketing information. All

of these facilitating systems are partially within the control of marketing. Finally, the external environment is made up of those forces which are not within management control: social, economic, technological, scientific, legal, as well as the cultural implications. Additionally, the demographic make-up of the consumer and competition must be taken into consideration.

Figure 4 illustrates this macromarketing system.

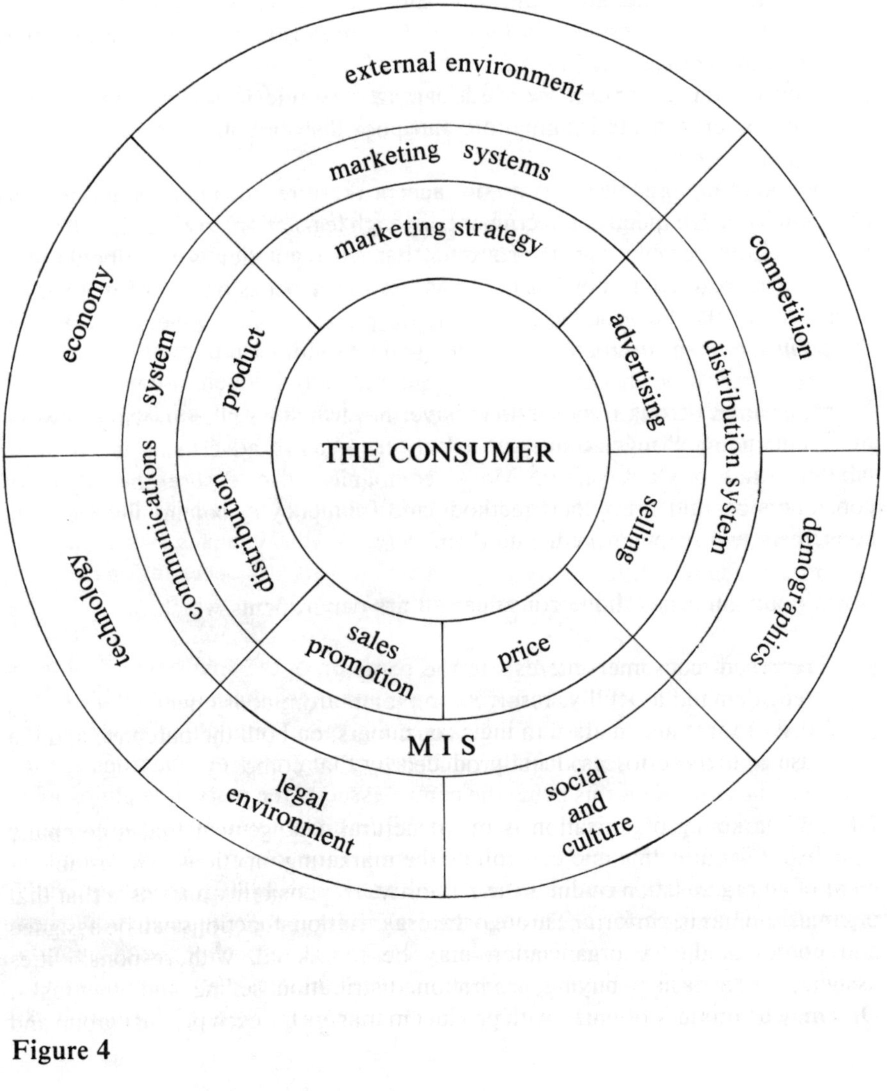

Figure 4

9 Marketing management has numerous responsibilities for protecting the rights of consumers in a business environment. In particular, it has a responsibility to ensure that certain consumer rights are protected; it must, therefore:

(a) carry out adequate tests to ensure that the product is safe;
(b) continuously provide the consumer with enough information which, of course, must be reliable;
(c) always give consumers an adequate choice of products to meet the differing needs of consumers;
(d) provide an effective feedback channel through which consumers can register complaints;
(e) in respect of the environment, ensure that they control pollution and be continuously conscious of the use of scarce resources in both production and marketing;
(f) always try to protect the disadvantaged people in society from higher prices, inadequate information, and poor distribution.

Many marketing organisations do not accept these responsibilities and tend to abdicate them in expecting government, through legislation, to establish effective controls. Common sense tells a marketer that self-regulation is much better than government regulation, but business has, on many occasion, failed to regulate itself adequately. Two good examples are the pollution of the River Thames, and the pollution of the atmosphere by the chemical industry.

Progressive marketing organisations have, nevertheless, been moving towards more effective self-regulation, particularly in areas of advertising to children, labelling and product safety. Many companies also ensure the rights of consumers by improving their methods and frequency of communication with consumers and helping to educate them.

Many companies now have consumer affairs departments which:

(a) represent consumer interests in the company;
(b) receive and, hopefully, resolve complaints from consumers;
(c) disseminate information to their consumers, on both the purchase and the use of the various products produced by that company.

10 A marketing organisation is the structural arrangement that a company establishes for directing and controlling the marketing functions. The establishment of an organisation outlines the authority, responsibility and tasks that that organisation has to perform. Through the organisation, functions can be assigned and coordinated. An organisation may be functional, with responsibilities assigned on the basis of buying, promotion, distribution, selling, and other tasks. Or it may be product-oriented with product managers for each product group and

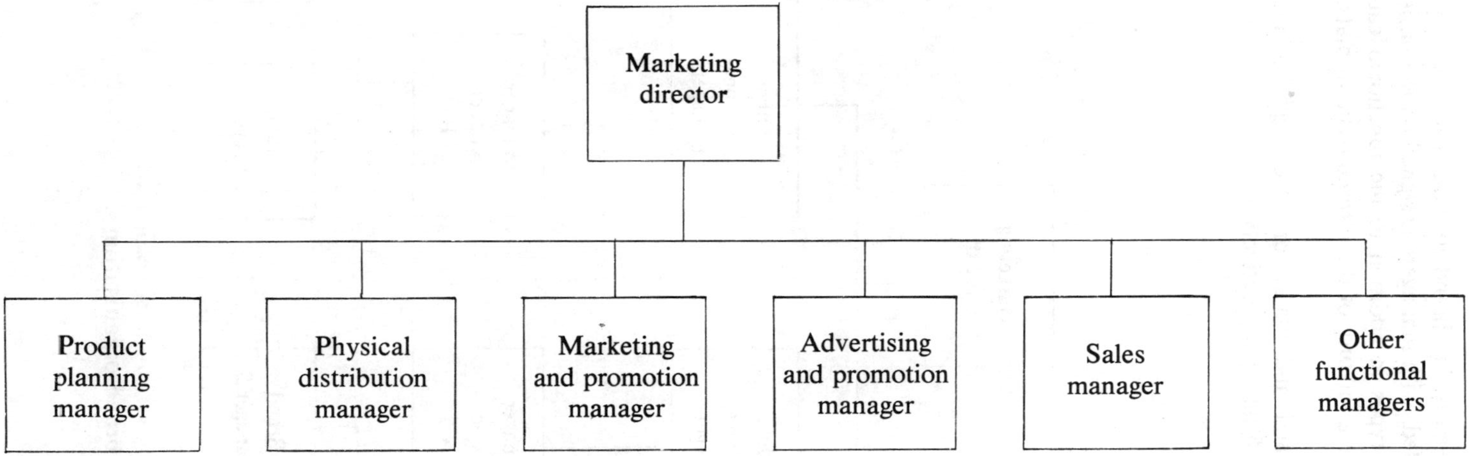

Figure 5 Functional organisation

brand managers for each individual brand, in addition to functional categories. Or it may be market-oriented, with managers assigned on the basis of geographic markets and customer types in addition to the functional categories. Many companies may well use a mixture of these three basic formats.

Functional, product/brand and market-oriented organisational formats are illustrated in Figures 5, 6 and 7 respectively.

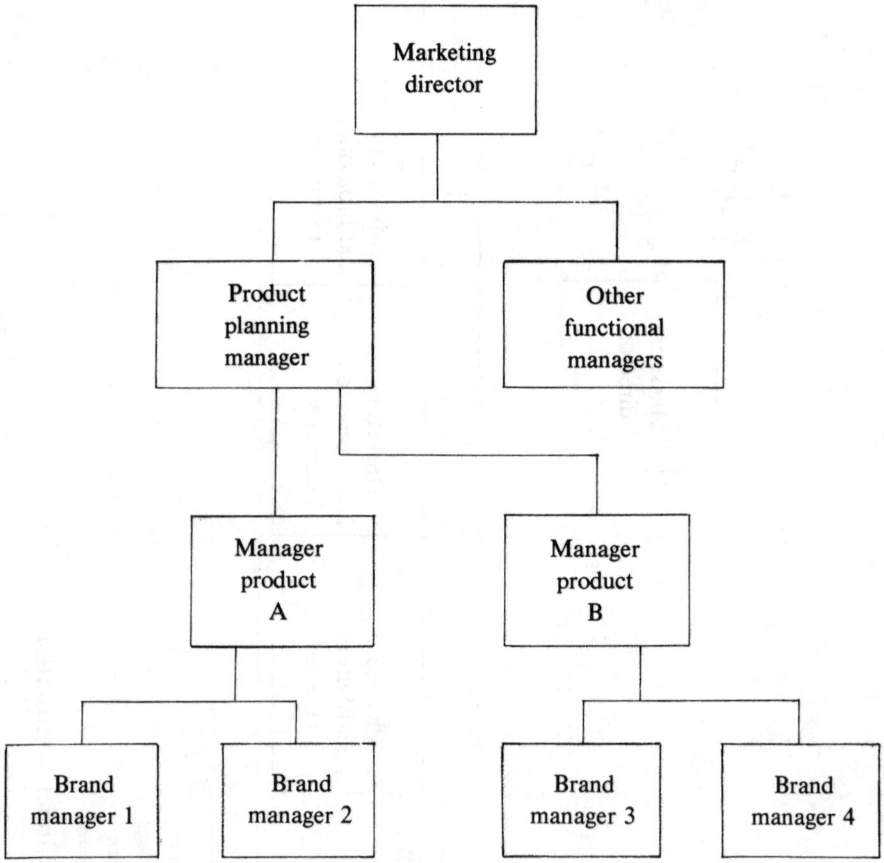

Figure 6 Product or brand organisation

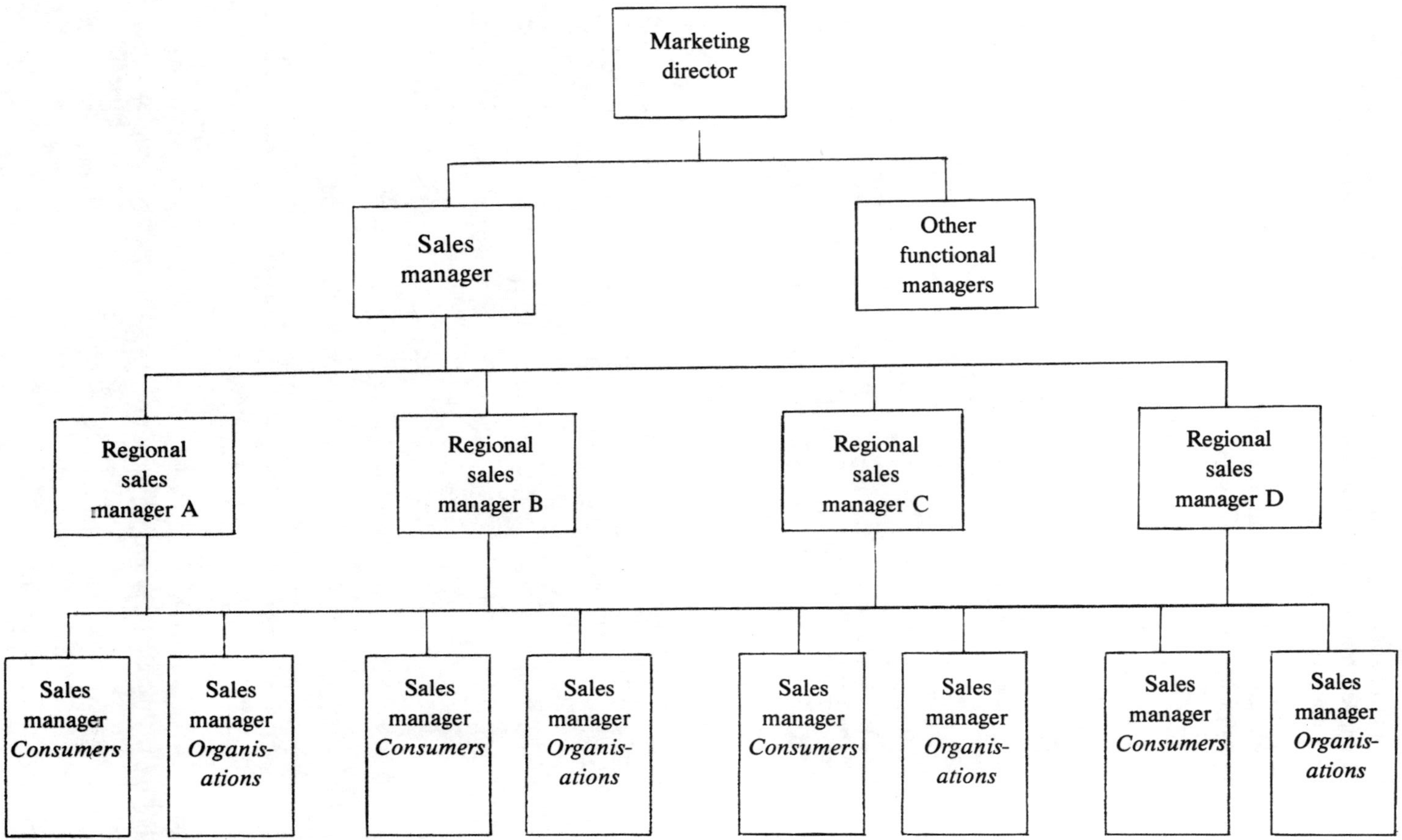

Figure 7 Market-oriented organisation

2 Distribution

INTRODUCTION

This chapter covers the subject of distribution. In includes the development and structure of the various distributive channels available; the functions of middlemen such as wholesalers and retailers; the relationships between the middlemen and producers; changes in distribution systems. It also includes coverage of the development of non-shop selling, mail order and direct marketing; the methods of distribution open to manufacturers; the management of the distribution function; logistics; distribution costs; and the role of the overseas agent.

QUESTIONS

1 'Marketing distribution channels are in a continuous state of flexibility and are constantly changing and evolving.' Discuss.

2 How does marketing management decide the number of distribution channels that should be established for a given product?

3 'Channels of distribution for services are usually much simpler when compared with channels of distribution for products.' Discuss.

4 How can effective distribution management assist marketing management?

5 What major improvements can distribution management make towards significant cost reductions in distribution operations?

6 Explain how the effectivness of the organisation of the physical distribution function can be improved.

7 Discuss the main types of retailer, and explain the major advantages and disadvantages of each.

8 What is non-shop selling?

9 A retail shop's exterior, general interior, layout and displays all refer to the physical characteristics of a shop, thus creating an 'atmosphere'. Why is this so important in a competitive marketing environment?

10 What criteria would you establish in selecting a distribution channel?

ANSWERS

1 It is true to say that there are very few certain factors in respect of marketing distribution channels, but of one thing the manufacturer can be sure: these distribution channels are in a constant state of flux and are steadily changing and evolving. This is not necessarily true for many parts of the world, but it is certainly true of the highly developed affluent societies. Manufacturers, middlemen, and consumers are continually seeking new and better routes to their markets and their sources of supply.

Physical distribution decisions are an important aspect of marketing strategy. Therefore, distribution policies should be the subject of very regular scrutiny and review. There are several factors that contribute to this need: changes that occur in product lines; new markets developing as unprofitable markets are dropped; changes that the manufacturers make in price, promotion, and after-sales service; a change in marketing objectives; new types of intermediary appear for a particular product mix as well as the possibility of the middlemen's function being altered; and finally, user buying patterns change.

After the Second World War, physical distribution channel changes occurred in several major consumer goods markets. In pharmaceuticals, for example, supermarkets and discount stores are tending to become major outlets for both toiletries, over-the-counter drugs, and some proprietary drugs; prescription pharmaceuticals, once filled only by chemists, are now filled by chemist departments within major stores which also sell general goods, including departmental stores and cooperatives.

Motor car tyres, formerly sold by garages, specialist motor car tyre stores, and petrol stations, are now available in discount stores, departmental stores, and supermarkets. Meanwhile, having lost a good share of the car tyre business, petrol stations have added not only seasonal lines of garden equipment and supplies, and recreation equipment, but also fast-moving food products. One large petrol producer has designed a petrol station which even provides push-button selling of over fifty convenience grocery items.

But it is the grocery product lines which have experienced the greatest changes in distribution channels. In the last two decades, the wide-product-line supermarket operated by supermarket groups and cooperatives has dominated the field (an innovation, incidentally, of outsiders to the trade and not, in the main, the same people operating before these changes took place). In the last decade, the established supermarkets have had to share the market with food stores operated in conjunction with discount houses. These establishments have not satisfied the needs of all segments of the market, however, since we are now seeing the expansion of convenience food stores which operate on a self-service basis in local consumer areas, carrying 2,000 to 3,000 different items as against the 10,000 to 15,000 items carried by supermarkets. Many of these convenience food stores also establish themselves by opening for very long hours, some of them from 7 a.m. to 11 p.m. seven days of the week. The newer and larger of these convenience stores are generally part of a corporate chain or a franchise system.

Wholesale sponsors of grocery voluntary chains such as Vivo, Mace and Londis in the United Kingdom continue to be in the vanguard of grocery distribution. Some of the leaders have developed corporate change to parallel cooperatives. Indeed, in the United Kingdom the power of the cooperative group has been steadily declining in the last decade. The corporate stores are usually placed in more competitive locations where the closer control exercised over them brings better results. Some of them have also entered the rapidly-growing institutional field in preparation for the day when they will be able to offer institutions an eating place or a fully fledged food service designed for the needs of this market segment.

One could also cite similar examples from other industries, but the message should be clear. Innovation in distribution channels is a major characteristic of affluent economies, and manufacturers and producers need a flexible policy in respect of distribution channels to cope with this. Companies that hold on to outdated distribution channels or which fail to see the potential in evolving new distribution channels are operating under a marketing handicap which may well ruin them.

2 How many distribution channels should be established for a given product is an extremely difficult question. But it should not be confused with the question of selectivity of or the number of middlemen to be used. This latter topic refers to the number of middlemen at each level in each distribution channel, whereas the question to be answered almost certainly refers to the number of different patterns used for distributing to the ultimate market. For example, a dual distribution system may have one pattern in which the manufacturer distributes direct to mass retail outlets and a second pattern in which he also, simultaneously, distributes through wholesalers to smaller retailers. Another example of dual distribution is the common one of a manufacturer distributing through agents in geographical areas which are sparsely populated or at a great distance from the production plant, and at the same time distributing to wholesalers or directly to retailers in densely populated areas.

Given that these different choices are open to the manufacturer, how should the type of middlemen be chosen to fill these different activities? When intensive distribution is the decided policy, this last decision area is, conceptually, simple. Basically, the company will try to sell to and through all middlemen who will buy the product. However, when the policy is one of some or complete selectivity, then a decision must be made as to which firms of a given type in given geographic areas will be selected to carry the product. The assumption here is that the manufacturer has complete freedom of choice, but this is not usually the case.

Middlemen may not wish to carry the product, even if the manufacturers wish them to do so.

Basically, the middleman must fit into the manufacturer's total marketing strategy. This means that the chosen middleman must be able to service effectively and have sufficient contact with a logical piece of the total market the manufacturer wishes to pursue. He then becomes one of the middlemen who, altogether, must service the total target market, usually with little overlap.

The strategy employed by middlemen must fit in with the manufacturer's efforts or marketing mix. The product mix and inventory policy, selling and promotional efforts, service and pricing policies must be compatible with the manufacturer's. Finally, the middlemen must have the requisite financial, human, and physical resources.

3 While channels of distribution for services are usually very simple when compared with channels for products, this generalisation is not completely true, as the following few examples will illustrate.

Agents With some types of services, agents may be employed to concentrate on the selling function. These agents are roughly similar to the agent–middlemen in the marketing of goods, and are usually classified as brokers or sales agents. This distribution channel is used in the sale of holidays and transportation, i.e. travel agents, as well as employment agencies. In some instances dealers may be trained in the creation or production of the service and then be franchised to sell it. Examples of this arrangement are restaurants such as McDonald's, labour offices and motels.

Middlemen With some types of services, although the actual product may not be transferable, tangible representations of the product are transferable. In these instances the market may develop institutional middlemen, even wholesalers and retailers. This type of distribution channel is often used in the marketing of securities and in some cases of life assurance, where a contract exists as a tangible representation of the service. Some service firms may market on a wholesale basis. For example, many laundries and dry-cleaners sell regularly through retail outlets to the ultimate consumer. The consumer actually has no contact with the company producing the service.

Convenience outlets Since services are generally not delivered to the buyer, the creation of time and place utility is a vital function in the marketing of services. Whether the direct sale channel is used, or whether some type of agent-middleman is used to reach potential customers, the factor of location with respect to the potential market will usually weigh heavily in the channel selection decisions of a marketer of services.

Geographical area The inability of most service firms to use middlemen to any great extent will obviously limit the geographical area that the seller can hope to reach. This emphasises the importance of good distribution channel selection on the part of the service marketer since he must attain maximum exposure for his service. Banks have come to realise the importance of this factor in recent years, and have initiated many innovations in the distribution of banking services, one of the most popular being cash-cards.

4 There is a growing realisation by marketing management that a highly responsive, reliable distribution system can greatly assist marketing efforts. It can, in fact, help in a number of areas, a few of which are suggested below.

It can assist in minimising out-of-stock situations through more accurate inventory planning and control, and thus lost sales due to being out-of-stock will be minimised. This has the double advantage of increasing both actual sales volume and the level of consumer satisfaction. The availability of stock is an important aspect of customer service, and the service reputation of competing suppliers is in many cases the deciding factor in determining which one obtains the business.

A responsive distribution system can help to reduce customer inventory requirements by allowing shortened customer order cycles, reduced lead times, and, consequently, reduced customer inventory requirements. To the extent that one company can develop a more responsive distribution system than its competitors, it will be possible for customers of that company to obtain an economic advantage by doing business with it. Such an advantage will undoubtedly generate more business for the supplier who has that capability.

A soundly conceived distribution system should help to solidify and perpetuate a supplier's relationships with his customers. This might be accomplished through integration of the supplier's delivery facilities and his customers receiving facilities, consignment of stocks to customers, and other devices of a similar nature.

Effective distribution can also assist in increasing discounts. The development of more efficient distribution procedures frequently produces sufficient cost savings to allow the investment of part of the savings in business development, in the form of increased delivery or quantity discounts. A company able to offer greater discounts will enjoy a definite competitive advantage.

Expanded distribution may become possible. More efficient distribution operations frequently permit more profitable and, therefore, more effective competition in distant markets or markets that were previously marginal. Expanded distribution leads, in turn, to increased sales volume.

Finally, an effective distribution system can assist in allowing greater concentration on the creation of demand. The development of a well organised distribution activity in which a separate administrative group is established to plan and operate the distribution system, will allow marketing personnel to concentrate more attention on their basic responsibility, the creation of demand.

5 Cost reduction opportunities in distribution operations can usually be found in one or more of the following types of improvements:

(a) *Simplification of the system* Physical distribution is primarily the movement and storage of goods. Therefore, the more streamlined the system can be made, the lower would be its cost of operation. A good example of simplification would be elimination of a food warehouse by supplying customers in the local market direct from the production unit. The result: one complete handling operation eliminated from the system.

(b) *A reduction in inventories* Frequently it is possible to reduce inventories by consolidating them at fewer locations, centralising the storage of slow-moving items, or shortening the stock replenishment cycle for localised warehouses. Reduced inventories not only minimise carrying costs, but also free capital for other uses in the business.

(c) *An improvement in packaging* All too often packaging designers and even product designers fail to recognise the practical limitations placed on design by physical distribution. Smaller, more dense, uniform package sizes permit greater efficiency in transportation and warehousing.

(d) *More efficient methods and procedures* Not only is it important to eliminate costs through the simplification of a distribution system, it is also important to ensure the attainment of maximum efficiency from whatever system is being used. This refers to the selection and use of the most efficient materials handling procedures and equipment, good warehouse layout and space utilisation, good warehousing and shipping methods and order processing procedures, and the consideration of alternative modes of tranportation and various types of transportation equipment.

(e) *The use of technological innovation* In recent years an increasing number of technological improvements affecting the distribution area have been forthcoming. These include such developments as containerisation, high-speed computers and communications equipment, air-freight, new and more automatic materials handling, trucking equipment suitable for both 'over the road' and local delivery service, and motor carrier distribution tariffs.

(f) *Revising channels of distribution* Depending upon the company's volume, its sales objectives and policies, and the nature of its markets, it may be possible to lower distribution costs appreciably by revising the channels of distribution being used, assuming that this can be accomplished without impairing marketing effectiveness. The marketing aspects of the problem are so closely related to the purely physical aspects as to be inseparable.

(g) *Reviewing the system for improvement opportunities* There is never any substitute for a complete, balanced review of the entire distribution process, all the way from the vendors through company operations to and through customer distribution operations. Anything less than such a total survey and total cost analysis will produce only limited improvement and can, in fact, lead to decisions that drive the company in the direction of higher total systems costs, rather than lower.

6 Responsibility for and influence over individual physical distribution activities are frequently dispersed throughout the organisation. This creates stresses and strains, since the production department is usually interested in longer and more stable production scheduling, whilst the finance department wants to reduce costs and inventory investments, and the marketing department believes it needs more inventory and higher levels of customer service. This segmentation of reponsibility for distribution and of influence over its major elements also makes it difficult, if not, impossible, to hold any specific individual responsible for particular cost elements, such as transportation, warehousing, or inventory.

In attempting to overcome this problem, many companies are moving towards consolidating under a single physical distribution manager all the functions associated with the distribution process. However, merely deciding which activities should be grouped under common management is not enough. Consideration must also be given to the form of responsibility, whether advisory or controlling, and to the authority that must be vested in the physical distribution manager to carry out these functions. Figure 1 shows the physical distribution manager: as a line administrator; with management responsibility for staff activities only; and with full responsibility for line and staff activities. The choice of which pattern of organisation to adopt can only be made after careful consideration of the basic nature of the business and the relative administrative capabilities of the personnel involved.

7 One can clearly identify six different types of retailer ownership:

(a) *The independent retailer* These independent retailers are distinguished by the fact that they operate one outlet only, giving very easy entry to customers.

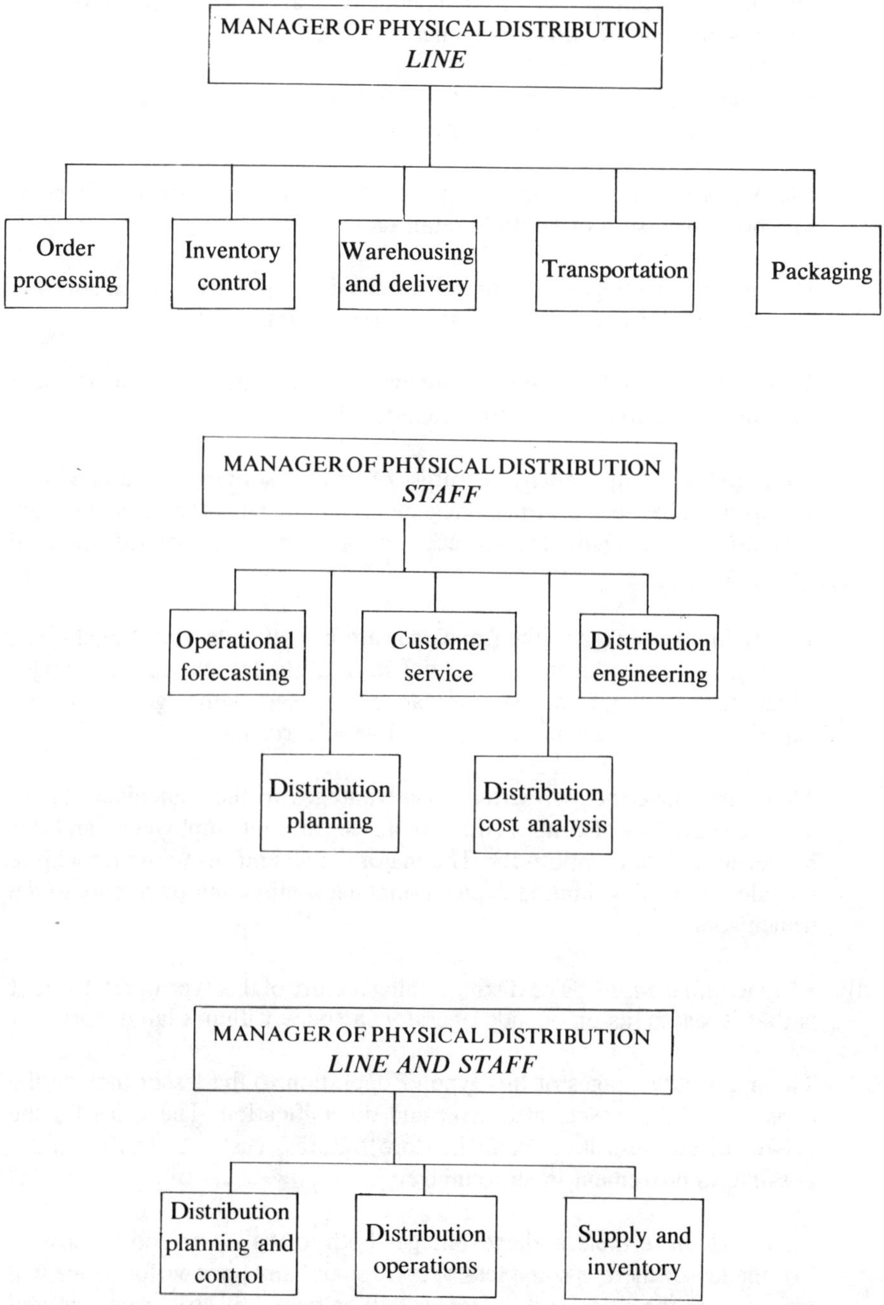
MANAGER OF PHYSICAL DISTRIBUTION
LINE
Order processing
Inventory control
Warehousing and delivery
Transportation
Packaging
MANAGER OF PHYSICAL DISTRIBUTION
STAFF
Operational forecasting
Customer service
Distribution engineering
Distribution planning
Distribution cost analysis
MANAGER OF PHYSICAL DISTRIBUTION
LINE AND STAFF
Distribution planning and control
Distribution operations
Supply and inventory

Figure 1

The major advantages of the independent retailer are personal service, convenient location, direct customer contact.

The major disadvantages are that they are faced with considerable competition, often poor management skills, and little capital.

(b) *Chain store retailers* such as Vivo and Mace. These are distinguished by common ownership of multiple retail units.

The major advantages are central purchasing, strong management, and specialisation of tasks, as well as a larger market.

Some of the major disadvantages are the lack of flexibility, high investment cost, and the lowering of entrepreneurial skills.

(c) *Franchising* The salient features of franchise are the contractual arrangement between central management (the franchisor) and independent business persons (the franchisees) to operate a specialised form of business.

The main advantages to the franchisor are investments from franchisees, faster growth, and the entrepreneurial spirit of the franchisees. The major advantages to the franchisee are an established name, good training, experience of franchisor, and cooperative advertising.

There are, nevertheless, certain disadvantages to the franchisor. These include some loss of control (the franchisees are not employees), and it is harder to maintain uniformity. The major disadvantages to the franchisee include strict rules, limited decision-making ability, and payments to the franchisors.

(d) *Shop within a shop* The distinguishing feature of this type of retail outlet is that it leases, as an outside operator, a space within a large store.

The major advantages of this type of operation to the lessor include the expertise of the lessee, little risk, and diversification. The gains for the lessee include less investment in store fixtures, customer traffic, and a possible improvement in store image.

There are, nevertheless, disadvantages both to the lessor and the lessee. For the lessor there is some loss of control and any poor performance will reflect upon the store; and the lessee will be bound by strict rules, limited decision-making ability and payments to the store.

(e) *Retail cooperatives* The essential feature here is that purchases, advertising planning, and other functions are shared by the independent retailers.

Some of the advantages are that independence can be maintained, the level of efficiency improved, and competitiveness with the major supermarket chains enhanced.

The disadvantages are that the individual members may have different objectives, the members may be hard to control, and considerable amount of autonomy may be lost.

(f) *Retail consumer operatives* These are distinguished by purchases, advertising, planning, and other functions, again, shared by consumer-owners.

The main advantages are that independence can be maintained, efficiency improved, and it enhances competitiveness with the major supermarket chains. There are also savings to members, social experience, and improvement in consumer leverage against some retailers.

Finally, the disadvantages are that it is difficult to organise, there is often a high membership turnover, and dwindling interest in performing the necessary functions of the operation.

8 Non-shop selling refers to retailers who do not utilise conventional store facilities. It includes such areas as vending machines, direct selling and mail order.

Vending machines use coin-operated machinery, eliminating the need for sales personnel and allowing round-the-clock sales; in addition, they can be placed outside, rather than inside, a store. Vending machine sales tend to concentrate in a very narrow product area. Cigarettes, confectionery, and drinks yield over 80% of all vending machine sales. Less than 10% of sales come from non-food items. Machines tend to require extensive servicing because of breakdowns, out-of-stock situations, and, particularly, vandalism.

Direct selling organisations sell direct to consumers in their homes. Cosmetics (Avon), vacuum cleaners, encyclopaedias, dairy products and newspapers are successfully sold to the home. This form of retailing can either be sold on a 'cold' canvass, on a referral, or on a party basis. In a 'cold' canvass, the sales person goes through an area, and knocks on each door in search of customers. With a referral system, such as Avon, past buyers recommend friends to the sales person to call on. In the party method, such as Tupperware, one consumer acts as host and invites friends and acquaintances to a sales demonstration in his or her home.

Mail order retailing occurs when the seller seeks orders through television, radio or newspapers, and receives orders through the mail or by telephone, delivering the merchandise to the customer's home. Very large percentages of consumer households in affluent societies make mail order purchases, mostly because of availability and convenience. There are general merchandise mail order firms, stores offering mail order as a supplement to regular business, as well as novelty or speciality mail order firms. The most popular mail order items tend to be ready-to-wear clothing, insurance, magazines and books. This form of retailing offers convenience for consumers, low operating costs, coverage of a wide geographic area, and new market segments.

9 Atmosphere is the sum total of the physical characteristics of a retail store that are used to develop an image and draw customers. The overall atmosphere of a shop helps to determine the customers it may attract, sets the mood for shopping, encourages impulse purchases, and sets a long-term image for the shop. Atmosphere is closely related to the strategy mix that a retailer selects. For example, a discount store will have ordinary linoleum floors, very crowded displays, centrally located cash registers, and trolleys to take goods to the car park. A prestige department store will have carpeted floors, wide aisles and attractive displays, recessed cash registers, and sales personnel to help carry purchases.

There are basically four components that make up a store's atmosphere: the exterior, the general interior, the layout of the store, and the interior display. The exterior of the store encompasses its store front, entrances, display windows and visibility from the street, its uniqueness, its location, the stores which surround it, and traffic congestion. The general interior includes flooring, colours, lighting, fixtures, wall textures, temperature, dressing facilities, lifts, type of personnel, and the convenience of the cash registers.

Store layout refers to the floor space allocated for customers, selling and storage, the grouping of products, the location of departments, and arrangements within those departments. Interior or point of purchase displays involve the types of cases and racks used to show merchandise, in-store advertising, mannequins, and wall decorations.

Recently the Safeways Supermarket Group opened an innovative 61,000 square foot food and general merchandising store in America. A major objective set by Safeway was to change the atmosphere consumers faced when entering traditional food stores. According to the store's designer:

> We set out to create something with pizazz, something that isn't mundane, and something which puts some fun and interest into shopping. There's a little less merchandise per square foot than Safeway would normally get into a store, but we've made it more inviting for people to come into the store.

To establish an atmosphere of this sort, organisations like Safeway would create a number of small shops in the centre of the store, using photographs to indicate direction, and set up a simulated café within the store.

10 After analysing the major distribution task, the manufacturer will have identified the most distribution channel options for his product. The question then is: which alternative best coincides with, and promises to fulfil, the long-term marketing objectives of the firm? To answer this question, each alternative is weighed against economic, control, and adaptability criteria.

Economic criteria are most important in making physical distribution channel decisions, since profits are such an essential marketing goal. In order to evaluate the economic potential of distribution alternatives, a company may employ a total cost approach. It will map out the distribution impact on each marketing cost that seems relevant, such as warehousing, stock and inventory, and physical transport. The firm will then attempt to assess the profit-impact of each distribution strategy, and select the most desirable alternative.

Unfortunately, this is easier said than done. It is no simple matter for the company to project the profits of a distribution system, even when it is has all the available information from intermediaries. Furthermore, in evaluating a number of distribution channel alternatives, it is difficult to obtain all the vital information necessary for the projection.

Among the many different difficult control questions that a marketer must face in weighing physical distribution channel alternatives, are: Will the self-interest of two or more levels be so opposed as to produce dangerous conflicts? Will the self-interests of two or more levels be so harmonious as to create an alliance against the producer? Will the channel contain any features that may represent legal problems?

A channel alternative sometimes seems ideal but carries a hidden danger. If it severely restricts the flexibility of the manufacturer, it may cause many problems later on as marketing conditions change. The producer who makes a 10-year contract with a sales agent may be stuck with that agent if a better alternative arises three or four years later. Thus, many producers are wary of distribution channel alternatives that require long-term commitments, unless the future of the industry is clear and marketing conditions are likely to remain stable.

3 The scope and value of marketing research

INTRODUCTION

This chapter deals with the subject of marketing research. It includes the scope and value of research; the importance of accurate data for marketing decisions; the need to monitor the behaviour of both users and consumers; the difference between marketing and market research, and the types and sources of information. It also includes coverage of primary and secondary data; the difference between qualitative and quantitative data; the limitations of marketing research, and the methods of collecting data.

QUESTIONS

1 Much research information is never used because the preparation of the report of research findings and its presentation is bad. What factors should a report contain?

2 'There are advantages and disadvantages in using personal face-to-face interviews in a field study during market research.' Discuss.

3 Sales information is a vitally important aspect of internally generated information. Explain how you would design and formulate a system that would ensure the best categorisation and use of such information.

4 The selection of the best market research company is very important. How would you go about it?

5 Describe the research process.

6 What are the advantages and disadvantages of secondary data?

7 An important component of the marketing information system in assisting it to identify opportunities and to assist in planning, is the internal reporting system. What contribution does this system make?

8 There are three main methods of collecting primary data;

(a) qualitative research;
(b) survey research; and
(c) experimentation.

Explain any *two* of the above methods.

9 The nature of industrial markets and the goods sold in those markets results in several differences in the way research is conducted and implemented. What are these differences?

10 The planning of the research design is perhaps the most important step in the entire marketing research process. How would you plan this?

ANSWERS

1 The report of the results of marketing research study should generally cover the following items:

(a) the objectives of the study and how the study came about;
(b) the principle conclusions of the study and possible recommendations for action;
(c) a review of how the study was conducted;
(d) the presentation of the major findings of the research study;
(e) conclusion, implications of the study, and possible limitations of the findings, in detail;
(f) one or more technical appendices containing information on the sample design and how the data was collected and processed, if primary data collection was used;
(g) one or more appendices of supplementary tables containing detailed statistical information drawn from the data derived from the study.

Not all reports are alike, and for a particular study the nature and organisation of the report may vary somewhat from the outline given above. However, in all cases the report should indicate clearly what the objectives of the study were, how the data were obtained together with some evaluation of the validity and reliability of the data, the findings, and how the findings relate to their original objectives. Recommendations for action may or may not be included, depending on the study and on the extent of the knowledge of the researcher of the feasibility of different action alternatives.

The results of the study will also generally be reviewed orally with the executives in one or more meetings. Initially a meeting is likely to be a very general one in which the researcher outlines what was done, indicates the major findings and problems encountered, and summarises the findings. At a later meeting, preferably after the executives have had the chance to review the final report, a more detailed discussion of various aspects of the study may take place, particularly in respect of the significance of the findings and of the implications for further actions and possible further research.

After this stage, it is essentially up to the executives to decide whether any further action should be taken. This is especially so if the research work was done by an outside organisation, which is not likely to be in a position to check periodically on what was done with the report. In any event, the primary responsibility for further action and implementation rests with the executive, who may, however, want to consult the researcher in making their plans.

2 The face-to-face interview conducted by a trained interviewer is the most flexible and, at the same time, most controlled method of collecting data. An on-the-spot interviewer can collect a wide variety of information. He can ask

questions, check in the kitchen, observe methods of storing and using products, take photographs, make descriptions, record on both cassette tape and on video film. The interview can be short or long and complicated, it can be structured or unstructured, it can be with one individual or in a group, it can take place at one sitting or over a period of time, it can permit a wide variety of devices such as pictures, advertisements, or products to be seen or used and reacted to. Personal interviewing also provides the ultimate form of control of the interview. The interviewer can ask questions, see the person answer them, and sense whether or not the questions are understood, whether the answers are perfunctory or serious.

The following points should be noted in respect of the interviewer. By and large, the research interviewer is a part-time worker, often a housewife who has had no formal training in the job. Door-to-door interviewing is physically hard work. It requires an ability to meet the public, get rapport quickly and an ability to understand a reply and to record its essence or record it verbatim. The interviewer must be able to ask a question as written without the slightest hint as to what answer she considers to be correct. She must have a business-like manner in getting on with the interview when the respondent wants to digress, and a determination to get to the next respondent. The job requires a willingness to push on in all kinds of weather and conditions, as well as high integrity, because the interviewer is out in the field alone and without supervision. Although it is a hard job, interviewers are traditionally low-paid non-professionals. As a result, the quality of interview is far from perfect, and there is a substantial amount of interviewer error.

The following situation regarding supervision in the field normally obtains. The interviewing supervisor usually recruits interviewers on a job-by-job basis. Typically, there is considerable turnover of interviewers from one job to the next. The supervisor's job is to train the interviewers, give them written instructions about the job, give them their assignments, tell them where they should go, whom they should interview, and send them out. In a few instances, there is some field supervision, but generally the interviewer is on her own. The supervisor maintains a schedule and sees that the work is completed and returned on time. Also, the supervisor checks over the work that comes in and usually makes an audit of a percentage of each interviewer's work.

One must also be aware of the indirect measures of reactions. Since asking questions may lead to interviewer error, considerable work has been done on securing reactions without asking for them. Observations of reactions of first-night audiences, for example, give the producers and performers clues regarding the show without directly asking for reactions. Researchers have developed many ingenious ways of securing reactions without making the respondents aware that they are being studied: these involve photographs of individuals watching television, fingerprints of people reading magazines and many more indirect measures.

Finally, group interviews: a very popular and useful way of listing attitude information from respondents is to interview them in groups. Replies are fuller, and there is a wider variety of points of view than is normally found in individual interview answers. There is another advantage: the marketer who has the original problem can listen to the interview process. He thus short-circuits the problematic communications link from marketer to researcher to interviewer to respondent and back again. There are disadvantages also: the quantification of results is hazardous; the sampling problem is difficult.

3 To design and formulate a system that ensures the best categorisation and use of sales information, it is necessary to assemble and total the different sales data in one or more of the following groupings:

(a) *Product* Practically all businesses that offer a variety of products for sale, and particularly those which have product profit centres, analyse the sales of individual products to determine purchase trends for each product or product line and the relative importance of each to the company's total sales.

(b) *Geographic territory* Knowing how sales are faring in individual territories is generally essential to companies that sell nationally or in large regional areas. And since in those companies the field sales force is organised on a geographic basis, the control of salemen and the lower levels of sales management calls for information about sales broken down by geographic markets.

(c) *Market segmentation* Companies that sell to a variety of buyers usually find it desirable to study sales to each of their several classes of customers, e.g. analysis by end-use, distribution channel, industrial and consumer products. For instance, companies that sell part of their output directly through their sales force and part through independent distributors, as a rule want to know the volume of sales made through each different channel.

(d) *The individual customer* For producers of industrial goods, a handful of customers often accounts for a large proportion of total product sales. In this situation, it is vital for the manufacturer to have facts and figures about the sales to, and the product requirements of, each of its big customers. This also holds for consumer product manufacturers who sell a significant proportion of their output to several large customers. A straightforward salesman's daily call report can be used for listing customers called upon, and divided up into different columns to record, for example: class of trade, direct or indirect order, whether it was a phone call or an actual physical call, whether the buyer was seen, and general remarks.

(e) *Sales unit* A company division, sales region, sales area, company-owned retail outlet, and salesmen provide groupings of sales data that are often automatically generated by product, territory, market, or similar classes of sales information. Which of the foregoing classes of information, or commonly which combination, a company uses in sales analysis depends not only on its circumstances with respect to diversity of product line, extent of geographical area, number of markets, and number of customers served, but also on such factors as the level of management for which the information is to be supplied, or the difficulty of obtaining relevant external data for comparison.

In an organisation with product groups as profit centres, top management is more likely to be interested in the total sales in each product group; whereas the managers of individual product groups focus attention on territory-by-territory sales, distribution channels, or end-use of their respective product. Top management may also be interested in the comparison between sales data for the industry as a whole and the company's sales, where such external data are available. In many instances, however, industry sales data either cannot be obtained or easily estimated or else they may be unavailable in groupings suitable for meaningful sales analysis by the individual company.

4 The following steps should be taken to narrow the field and help in making a proper selection of a market research company.

Define needs
Write down the exact requirements of the study. This written statement should include a general statement of the problem and an indication of the type of research probably required to solve it. It is important to indicate whether the research company will be asked to help to define the problem and structure the research, or whether the assignment will consist only of service type research, such as carrying out interviewing and tabulating results without any interpretation of such results. The type of research company to be selected and the price to be quoted will vary substantially depending on whether or not the assignment includes planning and interpretation.

Know the services available
Before making a selection, review systematically the different companies available. It is easy to fall into the habit of using the same research company for every project. It is also easy to rely on a general purpose research firm even though a smaller and more specialised company might produce a more meaningful solution to the problem. A good research director or marketing manager will not overlook as possibilities research companies which he does not normally use.

Previous experience
Satisfaction with work done on previous occasions by research firms is a most important guide to their use in the future.

Check references
If there is no previous experience with the company, it is useful to check with other clients. Do not hesitate to ask for references. Telephone discussions with others who have used a research organisation provide helpful insights into their capability.

Preliminary discussions
After the field has been narrowed, always hold preliminary discussions with those who qualify. It may be that there is only one organisation that fits the bill; if so, discuss the problem with this organisation. On the other hand, there may be five or more who should be considered. Discussions should be held with a reasonable number of prospective organisations.

Invite and compare different proposals
Based on the preliminary discussions, an informal proposal should be invited from those judged to be capable of carrying out the research. If the research includes planning and interpretation, the proposal will provide an indication of the care and form with which the research firm approaches the problem. The ability of the research firm to grasp the problem as stated, is a significant measure of its confidence to carry out the research. If it does not understand the problem, it is hardly likely that it will find a solution to it.

Quality of service research
If the work is of a service nature, it is important to analyse the quality as well as the quantity of the work to be done. Make sure that the sample selection will be made by scientifically correct procedures. Be sure that there are adequate controls over work in the field, that the supervision is competent. Find out quality of field interviewers used and how their work is validated. Pay a visit to the research company, if possible, to see its editing, coding and tabulating procedures.

Cost
The fee should be evaluated in the light of the quality factors. The cost of the market research study is usually so small in relation to the marketing expenditures that may be based upon it, that it is foolish to jeopardise the accuracy of the results by selecting a research company on the basis of price alone.

Which individuals will work on project?
Finally, ascertain which individuals are assigned to the project. Research work is done by individuals, not by companies. Find out who would actually work on the survey. Always beware of situations in which research is sold by one group of people and carried out by others without supervision from those who actually sold it.

5 We can divide the research process into seven steps:

(a) Problem formulation — much marketing research is undertaken to determine whether a problem does in fact exist, and if so, what its dimensions are. Once a problem has been noted and marketing research is requested, the researcher will need to know what alternative solutions are being considered and what information management need in order to make the best choice.

(b) Determining the sources of information — the second step consists of preparing a list of the information required by management, together with its likely source. The researchers should also make a search for the required data from secondary sources, including company records already collected.

(c) Preparation of the data collection forms — for field research the necessary forms for collecting the desired data must be both designed and tested. The starting point is listing the information needed. If an interviewing project is in order, a questionnaire must be developed which will elicit reliable information. The variety of data collection techniques that may be used range from a highly structured dichotomous questions to the use of very unstructured, open-ended questions.

(d) The design of the sample — the first task here is to determine the size of the samples. This has an important effect on the statistical reliability of the data collected, as well as the cost of the project. A second task is to specify precisely the universe from which the sample will be drawn. What groups are involved? How can they be defined? What geographical area or areas are being sampled?

Next comes the selection of the sample from the universe. While there are many ways in which this can be accomplished, probably the best way is the one that is most likely to produce reliability, i.e. through the use of probability selection methods, which ensure that each member of the defined universe has a known probability of being selected.

(e) The fieldwork — this step includes the selection, training, control, motivation, and evaluation of the individual members of the interviewing force. This is the difficult operation to control because it involves people who work alone, at considerable distance from the office, under considerable time pressure, and with a heterogeneous group of respondents. It is an important activity not only because of its cost, but also because the bias which results from the interaction between the interviewer and the respondent is potentially quite large.

(f) The analysis of data — this step involves editing, coding, tabulating, and analysing the data. Editing ensures that the sampling and interviewing instructions were followed, that all questions were asked according to instructions, and that the answers are understandable and consistent within the context of the interview. The data are then coded, or assigned to categories for counting, either by hand or by machine.

To a considerable extent, the problem and the information desired dictate the form of the analysis. An important activity here is to test any divergences to see if they are statistically significant or whether they could be due to random variations.

(g) Preparation of the report—no matter how effectively all of the earlier steps were accomplished, all would be for nothing unless an unambiguous report is prepared. Frequently it is necessary to prepare both written and oral reports.

6 The advantages of secondary data will be considered first. Many types of secondary data are inexpensive. Company records, trade publications government publications, and journals and periodicals are all inexpensive to use. Data collection forms, interviews, and experimental designs are unnecessary.

The assembly of secondary data is normally quick. Company, industry, governmental and library records can be gathered and analysed almost immediately, whereas the generation of primary data may take up to several months.

There are frequently several sources of secondary data. These allow a company to obtain various perspectives and large amounts of information and to verify data. With a primary study, limited data and only one perspective are usually obtained.

A secondary data source may contain information that the firm would be unable to get itself. For instance, a census study collected by the government could not be obtained by a single company.

When secondary data are assembled by an independent source in the market research industry, the results are believable. This source has a high level of credibility and a reputation for thoroughness.

Secondary data are helpful in situations where exploratory research is needed. Research of secondary data also often enables the researcher to develop a specific problem definition before collecting primary data. Furthermore, background information about a problem can be gathered from secondary data.

There are, nevertheless, certain disadvantages to secondary data. Available secondary data may not suit the purposes of current research because they were collected for other reasons; for example, the units of measurement may be different from what are needed. The company might require regional or local data, but the secondary information is broken down by county or country. In addition, secondary data may not be complete enough for the company, e.g. industry sales not collected by age, income level, and occupation of customers.

Secondary data may be dated or obsolete. Because the information was obtained for other purposes, it may have outlived its usefulness. The conclusions and statistics of a few years before may no longer be valid.

Details of the precision with which secondary data were collected, analysed and reported may be lacking. The company must attempt to determine for itself whether the data were compiled in an unbiased, objective manner. The purpose, data collection technique, and method of analysis of the original study should each be examined for bias. This is especially important when the source of the study had a special interest in the results. Supporting evidence should be read as well as summary reports.

The source of secondary data may not present all of its findings in public report, because it may hurt if competitors gained too much information. Generalities and omissions should be noted by the researcher. It is also important to distinguish among sources and rely on the one with the best reputation. Conflicting results reported by equally accurate sources may require the researcher to collect fresh primary data.

The reliability of secondary data is not always known. Many research projects are not re-tested. Therefore, the user of secondary data hopes that the results from one limited prior study can be applied to a current research problem.

7 The internal reporting system is designed to provide management with data generated by the company: orders, sales reports, marketing costs, inventory levels, distribution levels. These data are vital because they provide the basis for information on both revenue and cost in the profit and loss statement. Therefore, the internal reporting system is the basis for information on actual performance.

Sales information is the most important element of the internal reporting system. The firm must keep track of orders received; inventory levels; products delivered to wholesalers, retailers, and final customers; and prices paid. Because the distribution system is the source of this information, some firms ensure immediate access to orders and delivery data for their managers. For example, regional and area sales managers in many companies start their day with a report on orders and deliveries in their area of the day before. These reports might also contain percentages to compare with target percentages and the previous year's percentages.

But information on orders and deliveries does not easily translate into retail sales. For the industrial firm a delivery to a customer generally represents a direct sale.

For the most part, consumer goods companies do not sell directly to consumers. Factory deliveries are not synonymous with sales. As a result, most consumer goods firms have no internal means of determining sales result.

Because of the need for sales data, an important input into the internal reporting system is information about outside agencies. The two primary sources of sales information for consumer goods companies are store audits and consumer panel data. Store audits measure sales by subtracting their end-of-period inventory for a product from inventory at the beginning of the period plus any goods in. A.C. Nielson and Co Ltd audits a representative sample of many product areas including food and chemist stores nationally, and sells retail store information to many consumer goods companies. Consumer panel data use the periodic reports of a representative sample of consumers to measure sales. Both systems have their advantages and disadvantages. Panel data are sometimes subject to consumer reporting biases, yet they do provide information on where consumers purchase, what price is paid, and whether the product was bought on a special deal. Nielson data are not provided to management until three months after the reporting period. The delay often means management does not have time to react to changes in market condition. Another service has been introduced in the last few years to provide a quicker sales report. This is based on the withdrawal from warehouses. Although this system does provide more timely information, withdrawals from warehouses are still one step removed from actual sales.

8 (Although the question asks you to explain only two of the three methods, this answer will contain explanations of all three methods.)

Qualitative research
This does not involve directly questioning consumers or recording information. It is designed to get an idea of the problem. Therefore it is most frequently conducted in the early phase of research where the researcher is trying to form some hypotheses about opportunities or problems. Such information is most often obtained in focus group interviews, which are open-ended discussions moderated by a trained researcher. The group consists of 8 to 12 respondents who are asked to focus on a particular topic. When open-ended interviews are conducted with individual response, they are called depth interviews.

Another important type of qualitative research is projective techniques. These are designed to elicit information when the consumer might be embarrassed to provide it directly, or when it is too deep-seated or difficult to be expressed by direct questioning. Rather than asking consumers direct questions they may not be able or willing to answer, researchers give consumers a situation, a cartoon, or a set of words, and ask them to respond. Consumers are therefore projecting from a less involving situation.

Survey research
Qualitative research frequently leads to more definitive quantitative research. Once a firm has identified opportunities or problems and formed hypotheses, it

needs hard data to make a decision. The most important and commonly used type of quantitative research is the consumer survey. Surveys involve selecting a representative sample of respondents from the population of interests; developing a questionnaire; asking the sample questions in person, by telephone or by post; and analysing results.

Experimentation

In experimentation a researcher is trying to establish a cause and effect relationship. The most important cause and effect relationship is between marketing variables such as advertising, sales effort, or price, and sales results. To establish cause and effect, the researcher must attempt to control all extraneous factors, so that any variations in the effect can be attributed to the marketing factor that is being manipulated.

Assume a marketer wants to test the effects of in-store displays on sales. Two groups of retail stores are selected and displays are introduced in one group of stores and not in the other. The two sets of stores are matched for size, location, sales turnover, demographic make-up of the customers, and variety of merchandise offered. Percentage change in sales in the two stores is compared over a two-month period. In the stores without displays sales go up by, say, 5%, but in the stores with displays sales go up by 9%. Therefore, management concludes that in-store displays increase sales by approximately 4%. The cost of the displays is compared to the increased revenue, and management decides whether in-store displays are cost-effective.

If the stores were not matched, then the increase in sales might have been attributed to another factor. Assume that stores with the displays were in areas where competitive brands had lower market shares. Then the increase in sales might have been caused by competitive weakness, not the effectiveness of the in-store displays.

Experimentation is very useful in guiding marketing management decisions. It is used primarily to test specific components of the marketing mix to determine which is the most effective. For example, alternative packages, brand names, advertising campaigns, or product formulations might be tested on matched groups of consumers to determine which alternative produces the highest score for intention to buy. If the test groups are well matched, management should choose the alternative that results in the highest intention to buy.

9 These differences are:

(a) The importance of personal selling — industrial marketing relies heavily on personal selling because of the technical complexity of many products, the large size of many industrial buyers, and the need to communicate to purchasing agents, engineers, and production managers. As a result, a significant part of the industrial marketing research effort is devoted to identifying individual prospects and analysing sales effort. Such analysis is frequently based on secondary data and company sales records. In contrast, consumer marketers define prospects by identifying large groups of consumers as market segments. To do so, they require consumer surveys.

(b) Technical knowledge — industrial marketing research requires more technical knowledge because of the greater complexity of the industrial products. Therefore, industrial marketing researchers should have an engineering or production background, as well as marketing research training, to permit them to communicate with technical people in the company.

(c) Purchasing influences — a key task of industrial marketing researchers is identifying industrial buyers with purchasing influence. Several executives in the industrial buying company may influence the purchase decision. Moreover, the nature of influence may vary.

(d) Derived demand — the industrial marketing researcher is concerned with both the direct demand of the industrial customer and the derived demand of the final consumer. This makes the industrial marketing research task more complicated since data must frequently be collected for two types of customer.

(e) The industrial environment — the industrial markets are composed of fewer and larger buyers than consumer markets. Moreover, buying responsibilities tend to be spread across more individuals and to be better defined. Therefore, industrial marketing requires:

(i) smaller sample sizes than consumer marketing;
(ii) more extensive data collection in greater depth because of the complexity of the industrial buying process, which may lead to research that goes deeper into individual buying decisions; whereas in consumer research, data are collected by well specified questions on a survey basis.

10 Firstly, let us be clear on what a research design is. It is the specification of methods and procedures for acquiring the information needed. If the methods and procedures for the research are cheap or insufficient, the resulting data and findings will be inadequate or even misleading.

In the figure below, alternatives are shown in selecting a research design. In many cases just one research design (A1, A2 or A3) is appropriate. In other situations, an exploratory design may lead to a descriptive design (B1) or a conclusive design (B2). In some cases, the study will go through all three (B3).

Exploratory studies are designed to help identify problems, locate relevant variables and produce new hypotheses. Such studies must be quite flexible, since the researcher is somewhat uncertain about the exact nature of the problem. Hopefully, the exploratory study will generate data that suggests meaningful research questions.

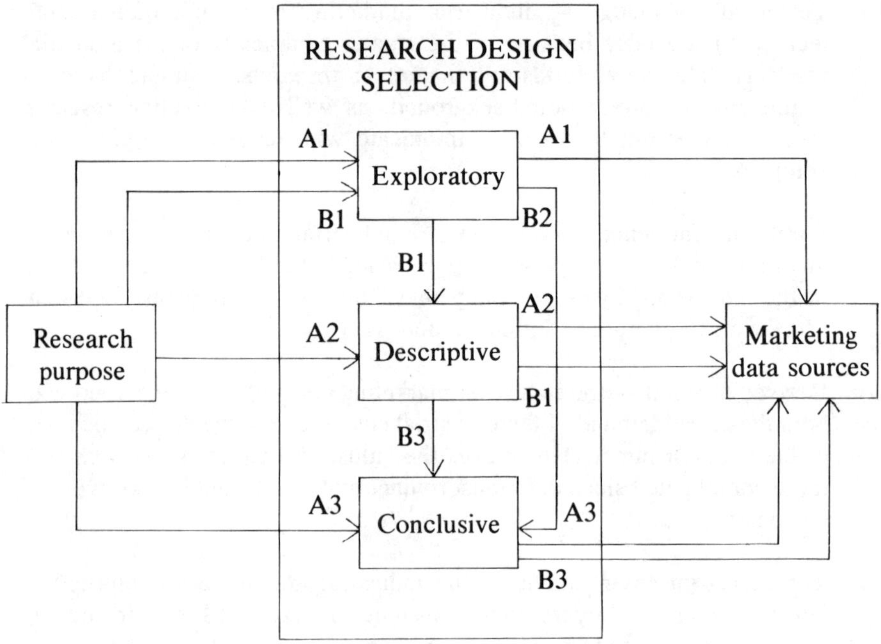

Figure 1 Research design selection

There are three principle stages in exploratory research. The first is the search of secondary information sources. Next come interviews with knowledgeable persons. After these interviews are completed, the research team will analyse them in two ways. They will study both the unique suggestions of each interview subject, and the aggregate conclusions that can be drawn from the majority of the samples.

The last stage is the examination of analogous situations, including case histories and simulations. Case histories help the researcher to focus on past marketing approaches to similar problems. Simulations, which are often computer based, involve experiments with a research model an actual marketing situation.

Some market research studies attempt to describe market characteristics or functions. For example, a market share study of the shoe industry may describe the share of the market held by leading competitors in men's, women's or children's shoes. A sales analysis for a shoe manufacturer may show the company's sales by territory, type of account, model of product and other variables.

There are three common characteristics of descriptive research studies:

(a) The association of two or more key variables — a sales analysis may break down the frequency distribution along various income levels. This can help the firm to develop predictions and marketing strategies.

(b) Specific research question — in this type of study, the researcher begins with a solid knowledge of a problem and clear ideas about hypotheses and testing methods.

(c) Planned and structured design — whereas the exploratory study is broad and somewhat unfocused, the descriptive study must be precise and systematic. The research design strictly controls sources of information and procedures for data gathering.

One of the important limitations of descriptive research is that it cannot establish causation, i.e., why something happens. A descriptive study may show a strong connection between two or more key variables, for example, a retailer cuts prices on stereo systems at one of its shops, and sales rise steadily over the next three months. However, it cannot provide solid scientific evidence that the price cut caused the rise in sales. Sales may have jumped because economic conditions may have improved in the area, and people felt more able to invest in goods.

In some research situations, a marketer feels a need for research to determine cause or connections. The marketer may not wish to change the marketing strategy because a descriptive study has resulted in suggestive data that may be misleading. Thus, marketing researchers may review the descriptive data, and then attempt to develop the causal relationship between the market factors with a conclusive study.

4 The organisation of marketing

INTRODUCTION

This chapter covers the organisation of marketing, the marketing department, and the coordination of marketing with the other management functions. It also deals with the allocation of authority/responsibility under the various functions of marketing, as well as the need to adapt the structure of the organisation to serve the differing requirements of the company's markets.

QUESTIONS

1 Describe the external factors that influence the marketing organisation.

2 What factors should be considered when deciding which marketing functions and reponsibilities to place at the corporate level or at the divisional level?

3 If a company decides on the 'product manager' form of organisational structure, what are the organisational pitfalls that can prevent its success?

4 Describe the basic types of sales organisation structure used for the salesforce.

5 In staffing the marketing department, discuss the advantages and disadvantages of promoting personnel from within the organisation as opposed to recruiting personnel from outside.

6 What is the systems approach to marketing?

7 'It appears that in the future the trend towards organisational efficiency will play an important role in the evolution of marketing.' Discuss.

8 Describe two different methods of organising the market research department in a company.

9 Describe the fundamental principles involved in the integration of the marketing function.

10 What are the organisational implications of the total marketing concept?

ANSWERS

1 The external factors that influences the marketing organisation fall into three main categories: business environment, markets, and the expectations and requirements of customers.

Business environment
The type of environment in which the firm must operate influence not only its marketing objectives and strategy, but its organisation for implementing them. For example, there can be considerable difference in functional emphasis depending on whether its products are marketed to individual consumers or to business organisations. In the former, the need to sell in mass markets and the struggle for shelf space in supermarkets tend to give advertising and sales promotion organisational prominence. On the other hand, industrial marketing organisations tend to put more emphasis on such functions as the level of service.

Another factor may be the nature of the particular requirements for success in a particular business. For example, styling and distribution in the motor car industries; cost control and selling a planned mix of products in the steel industry; and price, distribution, and product advantages in the motor car tyre business. These requirements relate to planning the marketing organisation because they point out the key activities that must be carried on and provide insights into what basic arrangements of activities are most appropriate.

A third environmental influence is the rate of change in the industries being served. If it is high, it may require more frequent changes in marketing organisation than if it is relatively low. The nature and lengths of the channels of distribution and the competitive structure are other environmental variables that must be taken into consideration.

Markets: their size, scope, nature and location
The nature of a company's markets has a strong impact on the type of marketing organisation that it needs to set up. Consequently, relatively few markets facilitate a market-oriented structure; a large number of market groups make a product-oriented organisation considerably more feasible. Markets covering a wide expanse of geographical area often require some form of geographical organisation; more compact markets may not require this. The number of customers, the frequency of purchase, the size of orders, the degree of after-sales service required are also determinants that shape the ultimate form of the marketing organisation.

Customer requirements
Certain developments in buying practices can best be taken advantage of by a market-oriented structure. These trends include:

(a) Increasing the central control of the purchasing function in some of the large companies.

(b) Allied developments such as annual contracts, blanket orders, and price protection.

(c) Pressures by very large wholesalers, giant retail chains, and buying groups for special deals and services.

(d) Unique buying and contracting procedures carried out by government.

(e) Customers' increasing interest in having the seller's salesmen deal with their problems.

2 In deciding which marketing functions and responsibilities to place at the corporate and which at the divisional level, management should consider the following points:

(a) The degree of decentralisation of authority — in a highly decentralised company, the division should control as many marketing functions as it can afford. Conversely, if centralisation is the order of the day, the chief executive may look for facts and guidance to his marketing director, who may perform a full complement of functional activities.

(b) The size of the division and the cost — large divisions may be able to support fully such functions as advertising and market research; small divisions, in contrast, may have to rely on the part-time services of specialists on the corporate staff for these two functions.

(c) Competence and experience of divisional marketing management — if limited, much more reliance will have to be placed upon the corporate marketing director to furnish service and guidance to divisional marketing personnel.

(d) Background of the division managers — if they come from functional areas other than marketing, the same point applies.

(e) Similarity of products or markets — product planning at corporate level may be justified if the divisions sell fairly similar products, even though the markets may vary. It may also be desirable to exercise corporate control over pricing. Conversely, if divisions make different products which move into the same markets, this may require corporate marketing policies and controls to ensure a unified inter-divisional approach to common customers.

(f) Central contracting for advertising — in those consumer goods companies where advertising takes the major share of the marketing budget, substantial discounts can be achieved by large-scale buying of television time and print media. Obviously, by pooling the requirements of individual divisions, the company increases its negotiating strength. Hence, in order to realise such economies of scale, it makes sense to assign such responsibilities to the corporate head office advertising staff.

(g) The need for corporate advertising — in most divisionalised companies, corporate advertising plays a useful role in conveying the image or personality of the company as a large, reputable, progressive, successful, and reliable organisation. To plan and conduct such a programme, to unify all forms of corporate communication, and to integrate divisional advertising, a corporate advertising group is absolutely essential.

(h) Top-level sales contacts — divisions may wish to call on the corporate group marketing director to help them in making calls on customers' top management.

(i) Diversification — the corporate marketing director may play an important planning and fact-gathering role in the company's efforts to get into business fields beyond those represented by the existing divisions.

3 Often the product manager concept never gets off the ground because of the company's failure to think through the specific management requirements of the product or brand. Even more often, top management fails to spell out clear-cut responsibility assignments and working relationships, as the following two examples illustrate.

One product manager with responsibility for a proprietary medicine found that he was cut off from direct contact with production scheduling and product development. Top management, applying a generalised concept of the job, had restricted the product manager's assignment to the marketing area. Yet the profit for his product depended heavily on maintaining uninterrupted production, even at a sacrifice in profit margins. Any product improvements were the major weapon for entering new markets and capturing the new business that would strengthen the company's competitive position. Without access to these functions, his role was ineffective.

A second product manager, for a grocery product, complained that he was virtually excluded from advertising decisions by the advertising manager who, having the ear of the chairman, was a very powerful figure in the organisation. Obviously, advertising was a critical factor in his product's success, so without the cooperation of the advertising manager, his attempts to plan the profitability of his product were nothing more than exercises in frustration.

Problems such as these stem partly from a failure to recognise the built-in difficulties of the product manager's job. To add to them by throwing road-blocks in his path could make a difficult job impossible. His success depends largely on how well he is able to develop and maintain a host of complex working relationships with other executives throughout the organisation. It is extremely important, therefore, to keep his channels as clear as possible. It must be even more important to recognise that each product manager's assignment must be tailored to enable him to focus on the particular activities that are keyed to the product's growth and profitability, regardless of what they are or where they fit in the organisation.

4 The following are the basic types of structure which are normally used:

(a) *Geographical* When a structure is developed on a geographical basis, it can vary from, say eastern regions and western regions down to small areas within a large city. Historically, geographic units have been organised by county or city boundaries. For better efficiency and greater results, however, the use of television marketing areas has been found to be more acceptable. Depending on the degree of company decentralisation, the selling group should be organised according to how many men the immediate superior can effectively supervise and control.

(b) *Industry specialisation* Principle guideline for the sales manager in this case is the type or the degree of difference between major customer classifications. If customer needs, use of product, and buying processes vary greatly, it is probably important to have more than one group of salemen. It is further necessary in some companies to assign one or a few sales representatives to handle limited customer groups or at times even a single account. The computer companies, for example, have assigned sales personnel to specific industries such as the motor industry, banking, etc. and sometimes to handle a single customer within an industry. This practice is not confined to large companies, as many small producers find that one customer provides more sales opportunities or volume than one man can handle.

(c) *Product specialisation* Organising along product lines seems almost unavoidable if the products differ to a large degree. This gives salesmen a better chance to become well acquainted with and well versed in what products they sell. This likewise means that the sales manager will assign larger areas for the salesforce to cover. But within that area, each saleman can become more strongly identified with his special line. Examples are numerous. A pharmaceutical manufactuer may have both proprietary and ethical lines, necessitating the two salesforces covering the same geographical area but calling on different buyers. A publisher may have titles for secondary schools, colleges, universities. In such a situation, a product line is so different that three different salesforces are required to handle the company's selling needs.

The combinations or variations of these basic structures are many and at times rather complex. Within the geographical region or district, a company can have both industry and product specialists. In some cases, a general sales force selling all products covers rural areas, and within the larger city areas, products are handled by industry specialists and product specialists.

A further complication is the situation where a company with a salesforce adds a new product line which is handled by the manufacturer's own representatives. A variation of this is where the manufacturer's representatives are used to sell the same products in lesser market areas or for a group of customers different from those being serviced by the regular salesforce. The sales manager must, however, be aware of certain legal aspects in classifying and serving customer groups as the complexity of the sales organisation grows, examples of which are sales of cigarettes to under 16s and the sale of drugs without prescriptions.

5 Generally speaking, companies prefer to promote from within but find themselves forced to go outside for certain specialised requirements, especially when entering new fields or when they lack an adequate executive programme. The following factors highlight the advantages and disadvantages of the two policies.

The advantages of promoting from within

(a) This is best for motivation and morale of personnel.

(b) It is less of a risk. Some companies feel that it is better to take a man with known weaknesses than to take a chance on alleged, but really unknown, strengths.

(c) The executive does not have to go through an intensive term of learning about the company, its products, and its markets.

(d) It is an excellent opportunity for executive development if done as part of a carefully planned programme.

(e) The executive concerned is less likely to 'rock the boat' and more liable to follow policy.

(f) Experience shows that a company generally pays lower compensation for any given position when promoting from within.

The disadvantages from promoting from within

(a) It means the company shuts the door to any superior outside executive talent that is available.

(b) It may result in loyal employees being promoted once too often, thereby losing a good man for a lesser position while failing to get an adequate man for the new position.

(c) It can create greater barriers to new ideas, since the man promoted may have a tendency, and even be subject to internal pressure, to perpetuate outmoded methods.

(d) Promotions may result from internal politics rather than merit and potential.

The advantages of recruiting from outside

(a) It provides experience and abilities for new activities not available from within. Some companies have recruited an entire team of executives to revitalise a department, or enter a new branch of industry.

(b) It can bring fresh thinking, different techniques, and new ideas to present efforts.

(c) It is often necessary because the company simply lacks talent capable of competing in today's market.

(d) It can help create a new and improved image to customers and shareholders. It may even be necessary to improve internal morale.

The disadvantages of recruiting from outside

(a) The new man might not be as good as represented or may not be temperamentally suited to the position or the company.

(b) He might adversely affect drive and morale of the executives.

(c) It might result in losing men who were deemed unsuitable or not ready for promotion, but still valuable to the company.

Every company sets a different value on each of the above advantages and disadvantages. However, careful consideration of all the points listed above should lead to the conclusion that the overriding factor must be that the best available man must be selected, regardless of whether he comes from the outside or from within.

6 The systems approach in marketing is really an adaptation of the principles used by the armed forces during the Second World War. It has been defined as:

An enquiry to aid a decision-maker choose a course of action by systematically investigating his proper objectives, comparing quantitively where possible the cost, the effectiveness, and the risks associated with the alternative policies or strategies for achieving them, and formulating additional alternatives if those examined are found wanting.

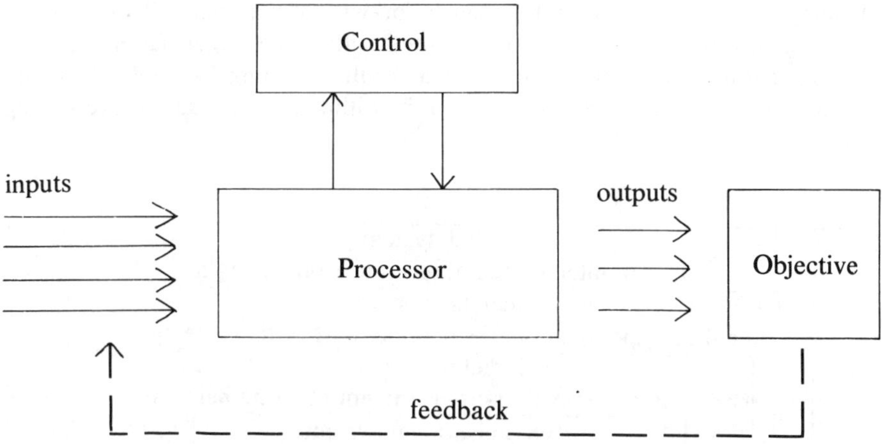

Figure 1 The systems approach

A model of the systems approach, based upon the 'black box' concept of the computer is given in Figure 1. In this model, the processor administers the operation. Inputs of products or product ideas are therefore converted into outputs. The objectives direct the process while controls monitor it. Feedback from both internal and external sources is the basis for further system change.

Unlike the closed and relatively limited environment of the computer, the environment of the marketing system is a large and open one, with many inputs, outputs and feedbacks. The marketing environment can be broken down into five basic layers, as shown in Figure 2. Each of the five layers in itself constitutes a system. The inner layers become the subsistence for the outer, or general layers, and outputs from one layer become inputs for the next.

The systems approach must help to focus attention on issues that are broader than are usually contained in any single aspect of marketing. It also provides for the logical and orderly analysis of marketing activity by:

(a) stressing marketing linkages both inside and outside the company;
(b) emphasising the relationship of inputs to outputs;
(c) highlighting changes in the environment;
(d) providing an approach for control;
(e) offering opportunities for innovation;
(f) providing a means of measuring results.

While the systems approach is particularly relevant to the analysis of managerial thinking in the organisation, it is a concept that one needs to use in the analysis of many other marketing activities.

7 The increased pressure for organisation efficiency has led to the development of the concept of total organisational planning. According to the concept, most planning is done in a central, organisation-wide department. Traditionally, planning has been delegated to one unit within the organisation, usually marketing, finance, or production. As a result, planning has not taken into account the needs and capabilities of all units within the organisation. According to one expert:

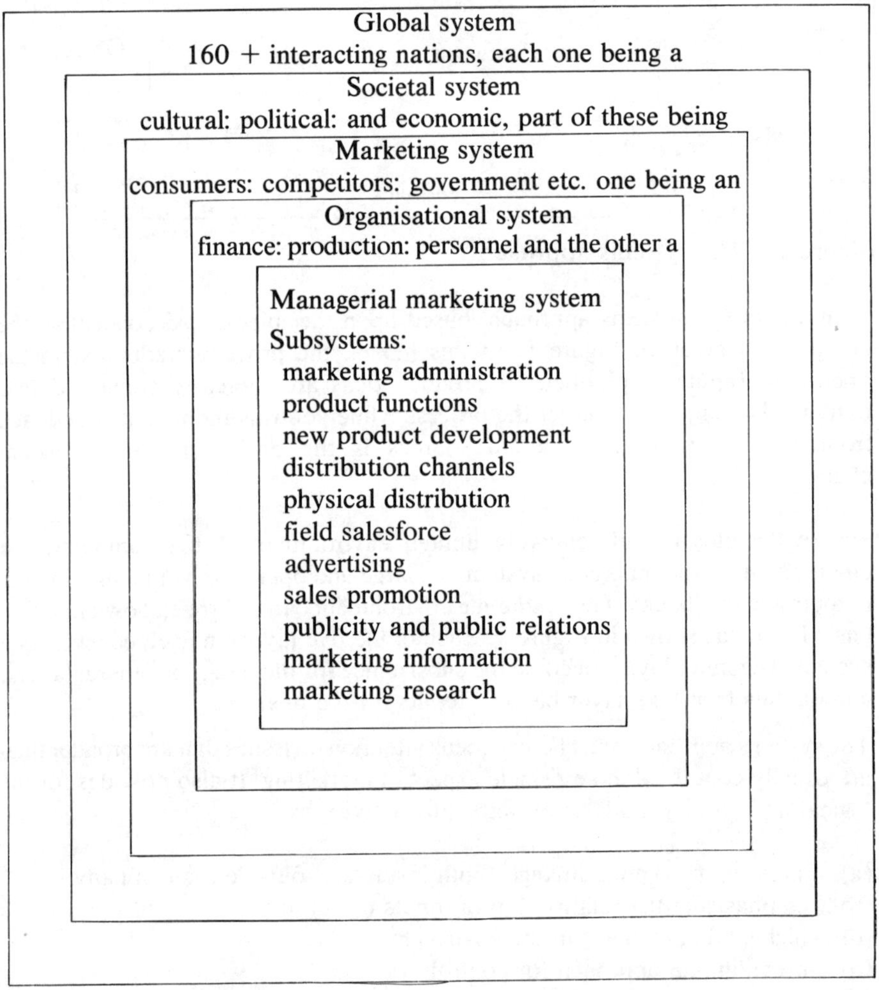

Figure 2 Global system

> Fragmented management is not only incorrect; it is unrealistically oversimplified. The true complexity of management is brought into focus when interrelated functional problems are considered simultaneously. The selection of a channel of distribution without computing the effects of distribution aspects such as purchasing, transportation, and storage, production costs and total net profits, is an unrealistic travesty of planning.

The movement towards total organisationl planning is also being accelerated by a growing emphasis on the financial functions of organisations. The scarcity of money in credit has made efficiency in planning imperative. In addition, marketing itself may become only a secondary cause of corporate growth. Large conglomerates today may owe their expansion to financial rather than marketing moves. 'Growth' has come to mean the acquisition of smaller companies, rather than the direct expansion of the organisation's own marketing coverage. The decision to acquire another company may be grounded in financial considerations, but the marketing opportunity and strategy must be sound for that company to prosper in the long run.

The scarcity of energy, raw materials and credit has also created a situation in which organisations are increasingly cautious about taking risks.

Finally, the computer has already had a major impact on the storage and retrieval of marketing information, and is bound to become increasingly important and useful in marketing operations. The computer's potential has scarcely been tapped in the area of marketing decision-making, where alternatives must be weighed under uncertain conditions. At the present time, the pace of computer technology is moving so rapidly that marketing people have not yet taken full advantage of it.

8 This question requires the student to describe only two different methods of organising a market research department in a company. There are, however, five basic methods of so doing and this answer will contain all five.

By brand
Under this method of organisation, there is a team of people at a level just below that of the marketing research manager, each of whom has continuing responsibility for marketing research on assigned company products or brands. While these people may go under different names in different manufacturing establishments, a common term for them is research brand managers.

With this method of organisation, the nature of the problem has nothing to do with the selection of the individual in the marketing research department who will run it. If it is a stated brand, the research brand manager on that brand will handle it.

The brand method of organisation is usually found in the problem-oriented department. In an organisation large enough to have both divisional and corporate marketing research departments, this is typically divisional.

By application

Here the department is organised along research application lines, with one individual responsible for copy research, another for media studies, a third for market studies and so on. This is really a basic method of organising either a division's research department or a corporate marketing research group. It is not too often that a manufacturer has the volume of research to permit this degree of research specialisation. Only a large company with a limited line can afford this: a cigarette company that has not diversified, or a brewery or distillery. Where this sort of internal structure occurs, this method may occur as an additional form of organisation, and is usually found in the larger marketing research department, parallelling specialisation that occurs within the marketing department. Where it occurs, it offers an environment encouraging originality and creativity.

By technique

In this method of organising, one senior researcher is a psychologist, another a statistician, a third an economist etc.

Sometimes the technique is a research technique, such as a sales analysis, store auditing, or consumer research. This method is not often found by itself, at least not in the department organised for problem-solving. As a primary method of organising, this method is better adapted to an exceedingly large research operation, or to a corporate marketing research set-up. In the latter case the group head of marketing research may well need the services of such specialists himself, and they can be made available as required for use by the divisional marketing research departments. The major advantage is that of providing specialisation and more sophisticated work.

By processing

This sort of department is organised primarily for the production of research data. In a survey-oriented department, it might consists of a statistics or sampling unit, a field unit, editing and coding, and typing and duplicating. This form is rarely found in a manufacturer's research department as a major method of organising because the typical manufacturer's research department buys most of research processing from research companies. It is inefficient, unless there is truly an exceptional volume of research, for the manufacturer's marketing research department to process its own studies.

Combination research group

Rarely is the manufacturer's research department pure in its form, because of its own special needs. Usually one form dominates, supplemented by one or more other forms. One manufacturer's marketing research department, organised along brand lines, may need a copy-testing group because it has developed its own unique copy-testing method and wants to control methodology and processing. In a smaller department, also organised along brand lines, a brand researcher — a psychologist — may be consulted on any projects requiring the use of psychological techniques, while another who is an economist will be consulted on economic problems.

9 Integration of the marketing function has often been mistaken as the primary, rather than the secondary, element of the total marketing concept. If the concept is understood and accepted by the owners and top management of a company, however, the integration of the marketing function is the logical and necessary step in implementing the concept of maximum success.

Integration refers to the combining of all activities related to the effective carrying out of the marketing function under the responsibility and authority of a single executive. Typically, such activities might include:

(a) field sales and sales management;
(b) product service;
(c) sales administration;
(d) marketing personnel;
(e) marketing research;
(f) advertising and promotion;
(g) product planning.

Depending on the type and size of the company, there may be other activities which properly belong in marketing. For example, some companies have functions such as dealer relations, customer or consumer relations, and distribution planning. In the textile industry, it is not uncommon for production scheduling to be part of the marketing department. In some other businesses, public relations, personnel development, and even long-range planning have been included in marketing's responsibilities, although the advisability of such delegation depends primarily on the kind of business involved and the type of overall corporate organisation employed.

Among the types of activities fully in the marketing area, some can be classed as predominantly line and others as staff. In a number of companies, the line or related activities are grouped under the title 'marketing operations' and the staff activities are grouped under the title 'marketing services'. Marketing operations normally include field sales, product service, sales administration, and marketing personnel; marketing services include market research, advertising and promotion, and product planning. Each company is different, however, and the best organisation arrangements require custom-tailoring to the individual company situation.

Where an integrated marketing function is established, very considerable skills are required of the executive selected for this position. It calls for a kind of vision, breadth of managerial skills, and leadership closely related to that of the chief executive. Moreover, in businesses where the total marketing concept is accepted, the person in charge of marketing should serve as one of the chief counsellors and advisers to the board of directors.

10 The organisational implications of the total marketing concept are fairly clear. Most companies that have adopted this marketing concept have realised the wisdom of an integrated organisational appproach to ensure a strong, unified marketing effort. Instead of allowing sales, advertising and other marketing functions to go their own separate, independent ways, these companies have designated people responsible for coordinating and integrating their efforts, in accordance with predetermined objectives, policies, and plans, to ensure that all marketing activities are conducted with the customer viewpoint uppermost in mind. In large, divisionalised companies this basic responsibility is exercised by a marketing director. It may also be implemented at lower echelons by marketing managers, product managers, and people with other titles but similar duties. In the smaller companies, the marketing director or manager assumes the role of integrating the various marketing functions reporting to him.

Obviously, the organisation levels at which the integration occurs, the gamut of functions involved, and the titles of the people concerned, will vary with the size of the firm, the scope and nature of the product line, and other basic factors. Nevertheless, the underlying principle is fundamental to building a sound marketing organisation.

Furthermore, under the total marketing concept, all functions of the business, not just marketing, look to the market-place for guidance. Therefore, marketing, being closest to the market place, must be so organised in relation to the other major functions that it can provide the leadership and direction that are implicit in acceptance of the total marketing concept as a way of business life.

5 Product planning

INTRODUCTION

This chapter covers the concept of product life cycle; product planning; design and development of new products; the stimulation of creative innovation; market segmentation.

QUESTIONS

1 What is a 'new' product?

2 'The development of a new product is closely linked to profitability for numerous reasons, such as: maintaining a flow of new products; being first in the market; and, by the experience gained on new product introduction.' Discuss these links with profitability in relation to the theory of product life cycle.

3 Discuss the sources of new ideas for products and services and explain the techniques involved.

4 How would you test a product?

5 There are three types of preliminary market tests for new products:

(a) controlled market tests;
(b) simulated market tests;
(c) sales wave experiments;

Write notes on each of these three methods.

6 Describe the total process of new product development.

7 Explain the concept of product life cycle.

8 What are the benefits of a market segmentation strategy?

9 Explain the difference between 'market segmentation' and 'market aggregation'.

10 There are basically three types of segmentation strategy: concentrated, differentiated and undifferentiated. Explain the difference between concentrated and differentiated segmentation strategies.

ANSWERS

1 A new product does not have to be new to consumers: for example, personal computers, disc cameras. It can be new to the company: for example, Heinz's introduction of a new line of canned soups did not represent a new product to consumers, but it was new to Heinz. Additions to existing product lines can also be considered new products to the company. Finally, a revision or improvement of an existing product can be regarded as a new product.

A leading advertising agency, Booz, Allen and Hamilton, studied the new product development practices of many companies and many new product introductions. They classified products by the degree to which they are new to the market and/or new to the company. Their research showed that:

(a) 10% of the products in the survey cited were new both to the company and the market.

(b) 20% in the research cited were new to the company, but known to the market.

(c) 7% were repositionings of existing products that were new to the market, but not to the company.

(d) The remaining 63% of the products cited were in an intermediary position. Of these:
   (i) 26% were additions to an existing product line;
   (ii) another 26% were revisions or improvements of existing products;
   (iii) the remaining 11% were new products that provided similar performance at lower cost.

One factor is common to these four categories of new products: the need for a new development and testing effort. Therefore, a new product can be defined simply as any product that requires a complete development, testing, and planning effort by the firm.

2 The link between new product development and profitability is illustrated in Figure 1. The upper curve represents the sales volume for a typical product over its life cycle. Products go through periods of introduction, growth, maturity and decline. The lower curve is the profit curve. During the introductory period, the firm is taking a loss while spending on advertising to create awareness and seeking to recoup research and development costs. If the product is successful, it will enter a growth phase in which sales are accelerating. The product becomes profitable. The maturity phase is marked by a levelling of sales. The effect of a slow-down in sales is magnified by the profit curve. The firm is still making a

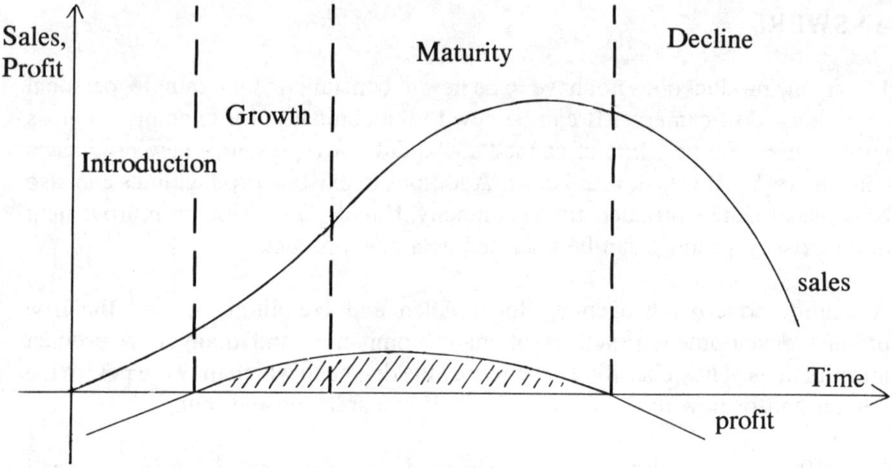

Figure 1 Profitability and the product life cycle

profit in the maturity phase, but profits are now declining and managers should be forewarned that eventual losses could occur.

The product life cycle should always be considered in detail. Its length and shape vary from brand to brand. Few brands experience such sustained growth that managers do not have to anticipate declining profit. The implication of the profit curve for new product development is clear: sustaining profit for long-term growth requires continual new product introductions. The company must have a planned programme that will ensure a constant stream of new products.

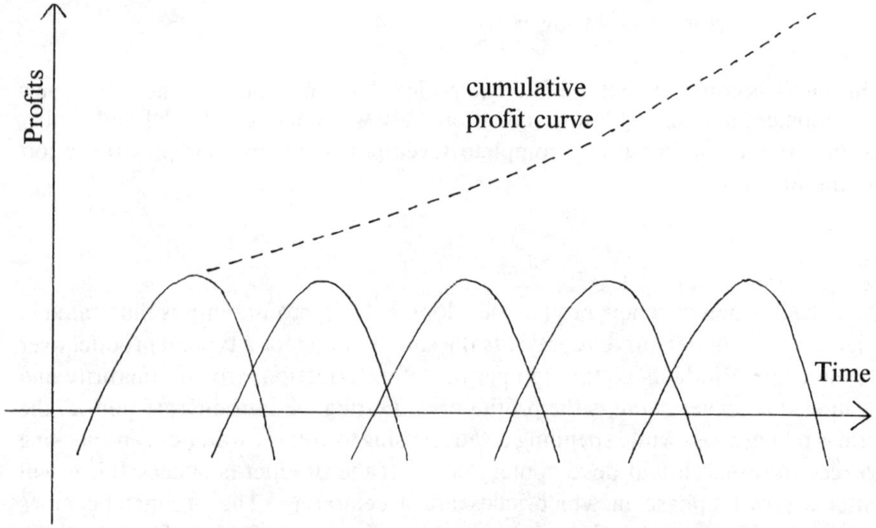

Figure 2 Effect of new product introductions on profitability

The effects of an on-going process of new product development are shown in Figure 2. A series of profit curves is depicted over time to illustrate successful new product introductions. A cumulative profit curve shows the firm's total profit position as a result. Profits will rise and eventually level off as the firm reaches the limits of its resources and as some existing products become a drain on profits and begin to decline.

We must also relate profitability and the costs of new product introductions. The Hamilton study mentioned earlier found that as a company introduces additional products, the costs of the introduction decrease. Specifically, the cost of introducing a second product averages about 71% of the cost of the first, a third introduction 71% of the cost of the second, and so on. This means that, on average, if the first product costs £1 million to introduce, the second will cost about £710,000, the third £500,000 and so on. Profits from successive new product introductions increase as costs are reduced because of the company's experience.

We must also consider profitability in relation to market leadership. An additional factor reinforcing the profitability of new product development is the association between profits and market leadership. New products that are innovations tend to be the most profitable. Much research has been carried on in this area, and one such study of 20 new consumer goods launched over a 15-year period, found that the first brand to be introduced dominated the market. On average, the second brand into the market did about half as well as the innovator, and the third about a quarter as good.

Finally, we must consider the success rate amongst new product introductions. Another factor that links new product development to profitability is the high rate of success among new products once they are introduced into the market. Much research shows that one can estimate the rate of failure amongst new products to be from 60% to 98%. But these research studies are referring to the high proportion of new product ideas that fail to reach the market. The Hamilton study found that once products have been developed, tested, and introduced, two out of three are considered a success.

Summarising, new product development is linked to high profitability because of the following factors:

(a) Once new products are introduced, they are likely to be successful.

(b) Such successes generate revenues for the company and ensure long-term growth.

(c) Successive new product introductions reduce the cost of development.

(d) Leaders in new product introductions in an industry are likely to be in a stronger sales position than those companies that follow.

3 New product ideas can come from many sources: research and development laboratories, management, marketing research, consumers, competitors, and many other sources such as the sales force, consultants, and publications.

Companies use the main sources of generation of ideas in the following ways:

(a) *Research and development* Many companies invest heavily to develop technologies that will provide them with a competitive edge. Investment in research development is not restricted to high technology companies. Philip Morris, the owners of the Marlborough cigarette brand, relies on its research and development to offer ideas for brands.

(b) *Marketing research* Surveys of consumer goods and attitudes frequently provide new product ideas. One company has used focus group interviews with consumers to develop new product ideas. Focused group interviews uncovered the need for a cold remedy which was efficient, yet free from the harmful ingredients used in many cold tablets. In another application, focus groups identified the problem coffee drinkers had with the bitter aftertaste in many coffees. As a result, one or two developed the chicory-based coffee.

(c) *Consumers* Generally, consumers are not sources for new product ideas. Some companies do however, encourage ideas from consumers. For example, IBM seeks out software packages developed by their users through an installed user programme.

(d) *Competitors* Companies try to monitor the new product development of competitors. Products introduced into test markets by competitors quickly become known to companies. Competitors' products can then be purchased and tested in company laboratories before the competitive product is introduced nationally. Distributors, wholesalers, and the salesforce are also sources of information, since they come into contact with many companies. Companies must make sure that executives are acting legally in acquiring the information on competitive products.

Idea generation techniques
Some companies have decided they cannot rely on the sources cited above for new product ideas. These companies have introduced techniques to ensure that new product ideas will be generated internally. These techniques generally involve company personnel rather than consumers, competitors, or trade associations. A group of managers, specialists, production personnel and any others involved in the new product development, come together and are given ground rules for idea generation. The most frequently used techniques have been:

(a) *Brainstorming* A specific problem area is defined. Ideas related to the problem are elicited in a freewheeling atmosphere. Wild ideas are encouraged — the more ideas the better. Criticism of ideas is discouraged.

(b) *Synectics* This technique was developed because some researchers felt that ideas generated from brainstorming were not thorough enough. A very general problem area is defined, and through associations with familiar objects, ideas become more specific until new product ideas associated with the problem area are identified.

(c) *Morphological analysis* A problem is explicitly formulated and the parameters of the problem identified. All possible combinations of dimensions of the problem are examined and solutions generated. The feasibility of each solution is considered. This method, for example, was used to generate ideas for new types of jet engine.

Other techniques have been used as well, but they all:

(a) establish openness and participation;
(b) encourage many and diverse ideas;
(c) allow participants to build on each other's ideas; and
(d) have discussion oriented to a problem.

4 Once a prototype is ready it will be tested to determine consumer acceptance. Product tests can be conducted:

(a) in a controlled laboratory situation;
(b) in shopping centres; or
(c) in the home.

Type of product test
Laboratory tests are sometimes necessary to control the situation in which the product is being used. For example, in conducting a taste test, it may be desirable to have a respondent pause between tasting several formulations of a product, to ensure no decrease in taste discrimination. Consumers can also be recruited in shopping centres. Many research companies invite consumers to caravan facilities stationed in shopping centres for product testing. This procedure permits careful screening of respondents, and also allows for the control of test conditions. Products can also be given to consumers to be used in the home. In the home, tests are the most realistic since consumption takes place in a natural setting. They also allow for consumers to use the product over time, and evaluate it against their regular brand. However, the researcher has little control over the way the product is used.

The procedures required of customers in product use tests are similar to those in concept tests: ranking of preferences for the test product and competitive brands; rating of the test product on key evaluative criteria such as economy, convenience, taste; and stating the intention to buy. The basic difference is that the consumer is being exposed to the actual product rather than an idea. Because of the greater realism in product use tests, sales and revenue forecasts based on intentions to buy are likely to be more reliable than estimates from the concept tests.

The product concept fit

A key issue in product testing is the degree to which the benefits described in concept are actually delivered once the consumer uses the product. The product concept fit can be determined by comparing the results of the concept and the product tests. For example, in testing an artificial bacon product, the company might develop a perceptual map positioning the bacon concept against three leading brands, as illustrated in Figure 3. The dots in the diagram show the position of the concept and three existing brands on four key attributes. The concept is seen as having fewer calories and as being more convenient. It did not have any particular advantage over existing brands on nutrition or its appetising ability.

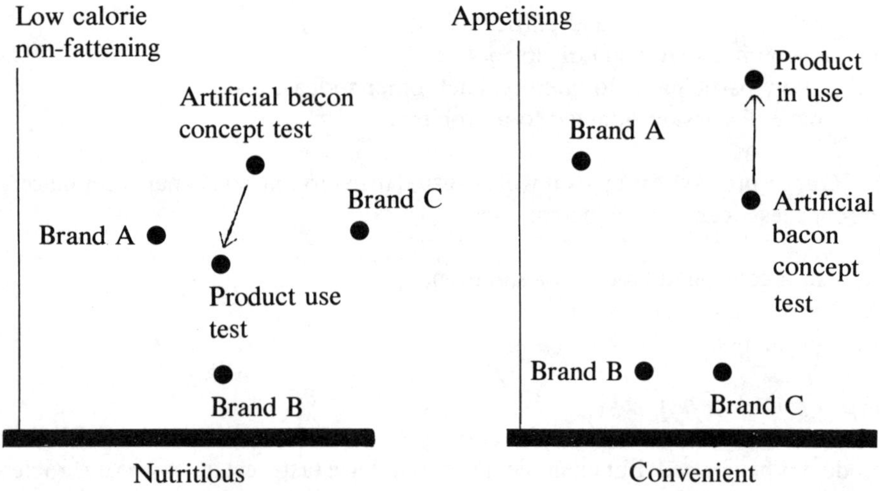

Figure 3

After the concept test, the artificial bacon product was given to those consumers who said they would definitely buy the product. The arrows in Figure 3 show the position of the artificial bacon product after consumers have used it. The perception of the concept deteriorates after it is used. It is rated more negatively on both low calories and nutrition. Consumers expected more of these key benefits because of the concept description that they perceived. The right-hand side diagram shows that there was no change in perceptions of the convenience of the new product, and consumers saw the product as more appetising in use than they were led to believe by the concept description.

Apparently, the concept description conveyed the impression of a nutritious but not particularly appetising product. When consumers used the product, they found it fattier but more tastier than expected. Since the product was meant to be positioned as non-fattening, the in-home test strongly suggested further product modification. The product could then have been sent back to research and development to be modified and retested. Further tests of the reformulated product could then show that it was rated acceptable on 'low calorie'. Sales and revenue projections could then be based on the last in-home product use test and might well suggest that introduction into test markets was warranted.

5 *Controlled market tests*

In controlled market tests, one or two test towns are selected and the product is distributed to shops and stores on a controlled basis. A market research company ensures proper distribution, and in-store promotions are carried out. The research company then tracks these in the shops and stores and themselves report back to the marketing company. In full-scale test markets, the company delivers the product directly to stores in the area with little control over in-store handling.

Controlled market tests are quicker and less expensive than full-scale test markets. They also provide the facility for testing specific components of the marketing mix. For example, two or three similarly matched sets of stores might be selected in a market, and variations in price or in-store promotions introduced in each set of stores. In one experiment known to the author a heavy advertising campaign was tested in one town and a lighter campaign in another. Two sets of stores were selected in each town and the product sold with and without in-store pricing promotions in each set of stores. Since distribution was controlled, the company could regulate the in-store promotion. The results showed that lower advertising expenditures in combination with in-store price promotions produced the greatest profits.

Simulated market tests

Several market research companies have established experimental supermarket facilities in which new products are introduced. Consumers are given a small amount of money and invited to shop in the store. They are told that they may buy any brand in the product category being tested, or they may keep the money. Before entering the store, they are asked several questions about brand preferences and attitudes and are then shown a series of commercials for the test brand and competitive brands. After shopping, the consumers are asked their reasons for buying a brand or for not buying at all. After enough time has passed to use the product, consumers are interviewed by telephone to determine what brand they intend to buy next, and are given an opportunity to go back to the store and purchase the new product.

This method has the advantage of measuring the initial trial in the supermarket and subsequent repeat purchase rates. Information on trial and repeat purchases has been used in models designed to predict market share very accurately. This method is also quick and does expose the product to competition as would occur if the product were introduced in actual stores.

Sales wave experiments

Sales wave experiments require the new product to be placed in the home. Consumers are asked to use the product and evaluate it as in the typical in-home product use test. They are then given the chance to buy the new product or competitive products at reduced prices. Consumers may be allowed to purchase up to six times. As with the simulated test markets, sales waves can be conducted inexpensively and very quickly. They can also be implemented before the final product and packaging decisions have been made. Therefore, they can be run early in the market testing phase. There are, nevertheless, disadvantages:

(a) consumers may be biased by repeated contacts;
(b) sales waves do not test advertising and promotional strategies;
(c) they are conducted in artificial conditions.

As with simulated supermarket tests, they tend to be used to support rather than replace full-scale test markets.

6 The importance of new product development and the risks involved have prompted companies to develop effective processes for introducing new products. While there is no specific blueprint for a new product's success, effective new product development requires the following steps:

(a) Identification of the new product opportunities — several approaches are available in identifying new product opportunities. These approaches use either unmet needs or unsolved problems as the basis for opportunity identification.

(b) Generating and screening new product ideas — new product ideas are generated from sources such as management, R & D, consumers, and marketing research. Once generated, these ideas are then screened with internal company criteria (such as company resources, market size, and growth), and external consumer assessment.

(c) Developing and testing alternative new product concepts — new product ideas that survive the screening process are then translated into concepts. Once developed, alternative concepts are then tested on consumers to determine the best positioning for the product and to identify the target group most likely to buy it.

(d) Developing and testing a new product — if the results of the concept test are positive, the concept is then translated into a physical product and tested. The actual product is tested in controlled facilities or by placing it in the consumer's home. Consumer evaluations of the product will determine whether the company will make a major investment in the production required for market testing and introduction.

(e) The development of a marketing strategy — management must develop an integrated marketing strategy for the product before introducing it. It is especially important to choose an effective brand name and package, since these components are so closely tied to the consumer's image of the product.

(f) Market testing — the product is introduced on a limited market basis to obtain the consumer's reaction in a realistic market setting. Market testing is the basis for projecting sales and revenues in the national market and often serves as the first step in a national 'roll-on' launch of the product.

(g) Business analysis — management must then attempt to forecast sales at each step in the new product development process. Revenue and cost estimates are developed to determine whether national introduction is, in fact, warranted.

(h) National introduction — once the decision to introduce the product has been made, the company must decide between a roll-on region by region launch and an immediate national introduction. Various components of marketing strategy must also be coordinated with the market introduction.

7 Figure 4 shows the traditional life cycle curve for a product. Naturally the sales curve will vary by product, but the bell-shaped curve is typical. The marketing strategies that are possible are given in the figure for each of the four basic periods in a product's life cycle. There will, of course, be exceptions to these strategies. For example, a brand may continue to be reinforced into the maturity phase. Some products are never repositioned or modified, and others may be repositioned long before they go into decline. However, the strategies given tend to be typical for each stage of the life cycle.

Stage 1 — Introduction
In this stage, the main purpose of marketing strategy is to establish the product or the brand. Product strategy is still in the development stage to ensure a high enough standard of quality for consumer acceptance. The main purpose of advertising is to create consumer awareness of the brand. The marketer must ensure sufficient distribution so that the product will be available in the store after it is advertised. When distribution is assured, discounts to the middlemen and cooperative advertising allowances are often offered to convince distributors to stock the product.

Pricing will follow a penetration strategy (that is, below the price of competition), if the objective is to make inroads into competitive sales quickly, or a skimming strategy (which is above the price of competition), if the objective is to maintain a quality image and appeal to a selected market. Penetration is the more likely

TYPES OF BRAND STRATEGY

MARKETING STRATEGY CONSIDERATIONS	Brand development	Brand reinforcement	Brand repositioning	Brand modification
Objectives	establish market position	expand target market	seek new market segments	prepare for re-entry
Product strategy	assure high quality	identify weaknesses	adjust, size, colour, packaging	modify features
Advertising objectives	build brand awareness	provide information	use imagery, to differentiate from competitors	educate on changes
Distribution	build distribution network	solidify distribution relationships	maintain distribution	re-establish and delivery new version
Price	skimming or penetration strategy	meet competition	use price deals	maintain price

Figure 4

strategy if demand is elastic and competition is intense. Under these conditions, the firm should price at or below the competitor's price, unless it has a unique product advantage. Penetration strategy will require widespread distribution facilities to ensure reaching a broad market. Skimming is more profitable if the company is directing its appeal to a smaller, select group of customers willing to pay a higher price. A skimming strategy assumes the product has some competitive advantage, resulting in price inelasticity and brand loyalty. Distribution is then more selective.

Stage 2 — Growth
In this stage, the basic purpose of brand strategy is to establish loyalty among those who would try the brand, that is, if sufficient trials were established in the introductory period. The main product concern is to identify deficiencies once consumers have had a chance to use the product over a period of time.

Several changes in marketing strategy occur in the growth stage. The advertising objective is to educate the consumer on specific benefits rather than to create brand name identification. As a result, advertising insertions will not be as frequent and will be more by way of giving information. Further, having won trade acceptance, the company is likely to cut back on trade discounts offered in the introductory phase. Prices may be increased, if the company followed the skimming strategy, to try to head off competitive entry into the market.

Stage 3 — Maturity
Sales begin to level off in the maturity phase because of more intense competition, technological advances which make the product obsolete, or changes in consumer needs. The most frequent strategy for revitalising the product in this stage, is repositioning to secure new market segments.

Greater competition frequently results in more difficulty in establishing a unique position in the market-place. As a result, marketers often have to rely on advertising to ensure market position. Advertising campaigns tend to shift from an information base to imagery in an attempt to differentiate the brand from a greater number of competitors. Minor changes might be made in packaging or product design, for example change in the colour of a product or changing the shape of the package.

Stage 4 — Decline
When sales begin to decline, the company must choose between totally redesigning the product, or withdrawing it. Withdrawal might be preceded by what some people call a 'harvesting' strategy to milk the brand for any additional profits by withdrawing all other marketing expenditures.

If the brand is to be modified, the main purpose of marketing strategy is to reintroduce the brand. This strategy requires the formulation of a new marketing mix. For all intents and purpose, the brand is treated as a new product. The main purpose of advertising is to educate consumers on the brand's improvements. Distributors may have to be convinced to stock the new brand, especially since sales have been declining. Trade discounts and advertising allowances may, again, have to be offered. Consumers might be offered coupons or price promotions to induce trial, since many former consumers might have been lost during the decline period.

8 The benefits of a market segmentation strategy can probably be best illustrated by research conducted by a leading advertising agency for one of its clients, a large food company. Sales for one of the company's products had been stagnant for some time, and had to increase to ensure product survival. The product was being advertised on the basis of its strong, distinctive taste. A study was conducted among non-users who expressed some interest in the product. Five segments were identified based on differences in needs and behaviour:

(a) impulse buyers;
(b) social conformists;
(c) bargain hunters;
(d) time savers; and
(e) health promoters.

All except the last segment were eliminated as targets. Purchasing behaviour of the impulse buyers was too uncertain to provide a basis for increasing sales. The social conformists were more worried about group norms than taste appeals. Bargain hunters were motivated by price, and time savers were concerned about convenience in food preparation, a benefit that was not the brand's strong point. Health promoters were motivated by health appeal, particularly for the family. Fortunately, the brand's distinctive taste was due to certain natural ingredients. A new advertising campaign was developed based on nutrition, wholesomeness and natural ingredients, and directed at the health food segment.

As a result of directing advertising to the health food promoters, sales increased, because most of the conditions cited above were met: there was a substantial difference in need orientation between current users of health food products, separate advertising campaigns could be introduced with no confusion or alienation among current users, and different media could be used for each group. A separate product offering to the health segment was not necessary but a different marketing mix was.

This type of research illustrates several benefits of a segmentation strategy:

(a) Segmentation can improve the allocation of marketing resources. The same amount of advertising expenditure improves sales and profits substantially when allocated to separate segments of the market.

(b) Segmentation permits a better identification of marketing opportunity. Without a segmentation of prospective users, health food promoters would not have been identified.

(c) Segmentation provides guidelines for developing separate marketing to separate target groups. The needs of the health food market guided the advertising campaign and their demographic characteristics and media habits guided media selection.

(d) Segmentation guides the product's positioning relative to consumer needs and competition. This type of segmentation study demonstrated that the product must be positioned as nutritional and wholesome to appeal to the health food segment. Such a positioning would distinguish the product from competition.

(e) Finally, segmentation provides guidelines for product development. Appealing to the health food segment did not require the development of a new product since the existing product had unique nutritional benefits. If this had not been the case, the company would have had to develop a new product to appeal to the health-oriented segment.

9 Most companies follow segmentation strategies, at least to some degree. But this has not always been the case. Until the mid-1950s companies did not generally direct product offerings to a specific segment. They directed a single product to a general market. This strategy is known as market aggregation, since it is designed to aggregate consumer demand on a mass market basis. Market aggregation does not attempt to differentiate between consumer groups but brings together different consumers under one product umbrella. Before 1950, such companies as Coca Cola, Ford and Chevrolet were essentially one-product companies. Market aggregation is appealing because it achieves economies of production and marketing. An individual product can utilise general media and large-scale distribution, and therefore enjoy lower per unit production and marketing costs.

Market segmentation, on the other hand, requires a more fragmented approach: several different product offerings directed to specific segments; separate advertising; sales promotion, and pricing strategies for each segment; and higher per unit production and marketing costs. In the table below, market aggregation and market segmentation are presented on a continuum and the differences between the two are shown.

Market aggregation	*Market segmentation*
Homogeneous needs	Heterogeneous needs
One or a few products directed to a mass market	Specific products directed to defined segments
Competitive advantage based on single offering differentiated by product attributes, advertising of price	Competitive advantage based on market differentiation
Profit maximisation by economies of scale in production and marketing	Profit maximisation by revenues from new products targeted to additional segments
Limits to profit maximisation are additional advertising expenditures	Limits to profit maximisation are additional market segments

The market segmentation is most profitable when consumer needs are relatively heterogeneous. The firm maximises profits by identifying segments with different needs and targeting products to meet these needs. Competitive advantage is based on differentiating market segments and directing unique products to each segment. The economic limits of a strategy of market segmentation are reached when targeting marketing strategies to additional segments is no longer profitable because these segments are too small or difficult to reach.

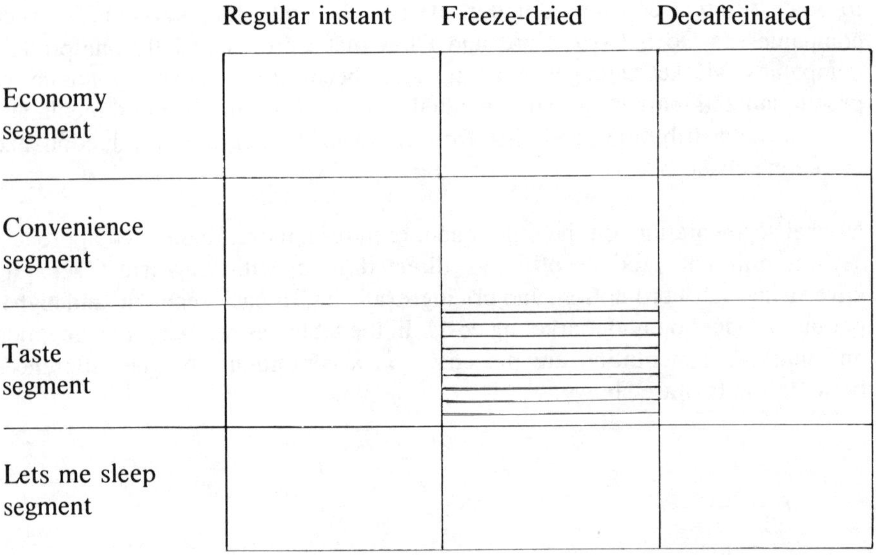

Figure 5 Concentrated segmentation

Market aggregation is most economical when consumer needs are relatively homogeneous. The firm maximises profits by selling one or a few products to a mass market. The major thrust of marketing strategy is to differentiate the company's single product offering from competitive brands by heavy advertising or a lower price. The economic limits of a strategy of market aggregation are reached when the company finds that the advertising and other marketing costs required to keep up with competition in a mass market are no longer paying off.

10 Concentrated segmentation targets a single product to a single market segment. Figure 5 illustrates this, using an example of an instant coffee market. The four benefit segments are listed down the side and three product categories across the top. The shaded area defines a particular product offering to a particular segment. In this grid, a company has only one product offering, freeze-dried coffee directed to a taste-oriented segment. A company with limited resources is likely to choose a concentrated segmentation strategy to focus its efforts on a portion of the market. It is aiming at a large share of a small market and is avoiding competition with larger competitors.

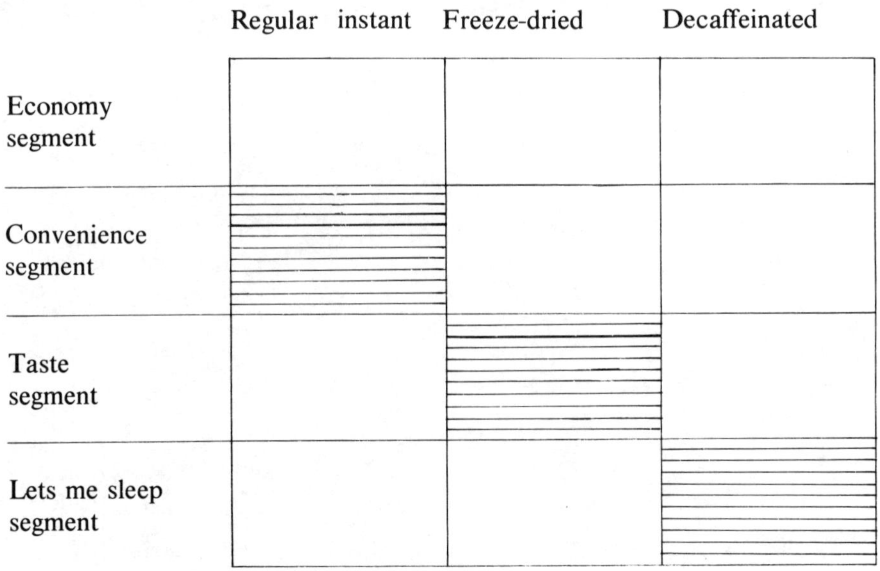

Figure 6 Differentiated segmentation

In differentiated segmentation, a company introduces several products to a variety of market segments; again the instant coffee market is used as an example, in Figure 6. The company, Nestles', follows a differentiated segmentation strategy for its instant coffee products, by offering regular instant, decaffeinated, freeze-dried and freeze-dried decaffeinated brands. It also offers a chicory-based instant to the consumer who wants a mild coffee. Each product is targeted to a different segment of the instant coffee market. By offering a full line of products to different segments, Nestles' has established a strong identification with the instant coffee category. Differentiated segmentation requires more resources since separate products and market strategies are needed for each segment. The greater marketing, production and administrative costs required in a differentiated segmentation strategy makes some firms wary of pursuing such a strategy extensively. The company must be aware of the economic criteria that apply: continue to segment on a differentiated basis as long as the marginal revenue gained from marketing to each additional segment is greater than the marginal cost of adding that segment. Companies have occasionally over-segmented their markets by fragmenting their resources to the point where marketing to additional segments is no longer profitable.

6 Pricing

INTRODUCTION

This chapter contains questions and answers in respect of pricing and the dimensions of pricing policy and strategies; pricing methods; pricing structures; and price competitions. It also covers the administration of changes in price.

QUESTIONS

1 Describe the consumer's conception of price.

2 What areas would you consider pursuing if your pricing objectives were volume-oriented.

3 Describe the internal organisational factors that can affect the price of products.

4 How would you attempt to decide upon a strategy for pricing your product?

5 What do you understand by the term 'Market segmentation pricing'?

6 How would you price a new product?

7 'Price flexibility is determined by the options in the price structure that raise or lower the price.' Discuss.

8 How would you initiate a price change?

9 What is the relationship between promotion and price, and between distribution and price?

10 How would you price a product in the maturity stage of its life cycle?

ANSWERS

1 Consumers view price in various ways according to their buying behaviour. Their perceptions of price and the benefits that they obtain from it may be categorised as follows:

The value of the total marketing offering
Marketers want to know what value particular segments of the market will place on the company's product offering. In other words, they need to know what volume of goods can be sold at a given price. Marketers must also know the relationship between price changes and consumer demand.

The effect of affluence
Because of rising incomes and a high level of discretionary spending over the past few decades, consumers are enjoying a wider range of products and services than ever before. This includes an increase both in durable goods, such as fridge-freezers and colour televisions, and in convenience products. The general effect has been to desensitise consumers to specific prices and to make price comparisons less important.

Price consciousness
Many research surveys suggest that a very large percentage of consumers remember a price that they paid for food products, and the majority of these recall the correct price. Price consciousness appears to be inversely correlated with social class. The more affluent consumers are, the less likely they are to be conscious of prices. Price consciousness varies greatly from item to item, but generally is lower for brand name items.

The importance of price
Market research indicates that the brand name may be more important than price in consumer purchases of most food products and drinks. In clothing purchases consumers are influenced by price, but the fit, style and quality appear to be even more important.

Price standards and ranges
Buyers often have ranges of acceptable prices for a particular purchase, and will reject any price that is outside that range. In many cases buyers will become accustomed to a standard price that functions as a yardstick for evaluating new products.

Price as a quality indicator
The relationship between price and quality is of great interest to marketing men. Consumers may purchase more of the company's product if the price is high rather than low, probably because of increased prestige of the product, or because consumers genuinely believe higher prices mean better quality. In the motor car tyre replacement market, for example, product quality is directly related to price.

It is also true, however, that prices are often a monetary expression of the opinions and buying patterns of uninformed consumers.

2 The areas marketers should consider pursuing if pricing objectives are volume-oriented are as follows:

(a) The maximisation of sales revenue — many businesses have traditionally pursued maximum sales revenue through high volume of sales. Conventional wisdom has dictated that sales growth was a positive business indicator, that high sales led inevitably to high profits, and that high production levels built a sizeable workforce. However, recession and economic shortages have resulted in a re-examination of this volume-oriented thinking. Companies have realised that sales growth does not necessarily lead to higher profits. Certain product lines with high marginal costs may be popular with consumers, but may yield only limited profits for the company.

(b) Maximisation of market share — the pricing policy of some companies is geared towards maximising the company's market share. When volume is increasing but the company's competitors are multiplying at an even faster rate, a false sense of security may develop. To offset this danger, companies keep a close watch on their percentage of the market share. In the field of pocket calculators, companies such as Texas Instruments, Casio, Sinclair, and Hewlett Packard, all reduce their prices in order to increase their share of the market.

(c) Maximisation of customer volume — a business company may elect to offer an unusually low price in order to increase dramatically the number of customers using the product. This is known as a rapid penetration objective. The company hopes to increase its share of the market through this strategy.

Non-profit organisations in particular often set low prices in order to increase awareness and acceptance of their products and services. An environmental protection group may distribute its literature at a low cost, or even free. The aim is to circulate the material and to build knowledge of the issues and of the organisation's programme.

(d) Minimisation of customer volume — there are sometimes unusual circumstances in which a company wants to discourage the public, or certain segments of the public, from using its product or service. This dilemma has become more common in recent years because of the energy crises and the growing international pollution problems. Many major towns and cities want to limit the number of motor cars using roads and bridges and entering the central business area from the suburbs. Therefore, bridge tolls and tunnel tolls are raised and car parking rates increase tremendously.

3 There are a considerable number of internal forces that can affect pricing considerations. These include: pricing objectives, product characteristics, and costs, which can be controlled by the company itself. By contrast, the external forces, such as suppliers, competitors, legal and ethical constraints, cannot be controlled in any meaningful way. These internal and external pressures narrow the latitude that the company has in making its final pricing decision. In some cases, the company may have virtually no choice at all, especially when it must attempt to meet or undercut competition.

Objectives

The variety of possible pricing objectives is fairly wide. The influence of these objectives depends upon how well defined they are, especially in quantitative terms, for example, a 15% increase in sales. Setting specific objectives for each product permits the multi-product marketer to compare performance among products.

Organisation

There are two basic levels of pricing decision. A company will decide on its overall price strategies, and these will be used to determine particular price strategies. The other function, known as the mechanics of pricing, may be handled at lower levels of a company's organisational hierarchy. But the firm's overall pricing strategies are discussed and decided at a high level, perhaps by the board of directors or at least by a committee of senior executives.

Pricing organisation varies widely

In some companies, production and marketing specialists have an important say in the pricing process. In others, computer print-outs have become a vital instrument. Some companies with nationwide enterprises conduct pricing on a centralised basis, while others rely on lower and middle management personnel as part of a more decentralised price-setting system.

Marketing mix

Marketing experts see price as only one of many important elements in a marketing mix. A pricing decision must be understood as one integrated element of a total marketing strategy and must be coordinated within the framework of this overall strategy.

In some industries, a company may use price-cutting as a marketing technique. Other companies may raise prices as a deliberate strategy to build a high-prestige product line. In either case, the effort will not succeed unless the price manipulation is combined with a total marketing strategy which supports the price change. Thus, a company that raises its prices may add a more impressive looking package and may begin a new advertising campaign. If it increases its prices without this kind of total marketing effort, the results may be disastrous.

Product differentiation
Generally, the more a company's product is differentiated from competitive offerings, the more leeway it has in setting prices. If the public sees all fast-food cafes and restaurants as identical, it would be difficult for any company to deviate sharply from the common price level. When a company cannot differentiate its product easily from its competitors, it may choose to differentiate the image of the entire organisation by building a solid reputation among customers.

Costs
Costs are often a misunderstood factor in pricing. There are two common misconceptions. Because people know that prices should generally cover costs, conventional wisdom holds that costs are the chief fact in pricing. Yet, while prices must absorb costs in the long run, factors other than costs may be the prime influence in the short term.

It is generally assumed that costs are a price-determining factor. Actually, the reverse may be true; prices may be a cost-determining factor. A firm may decide

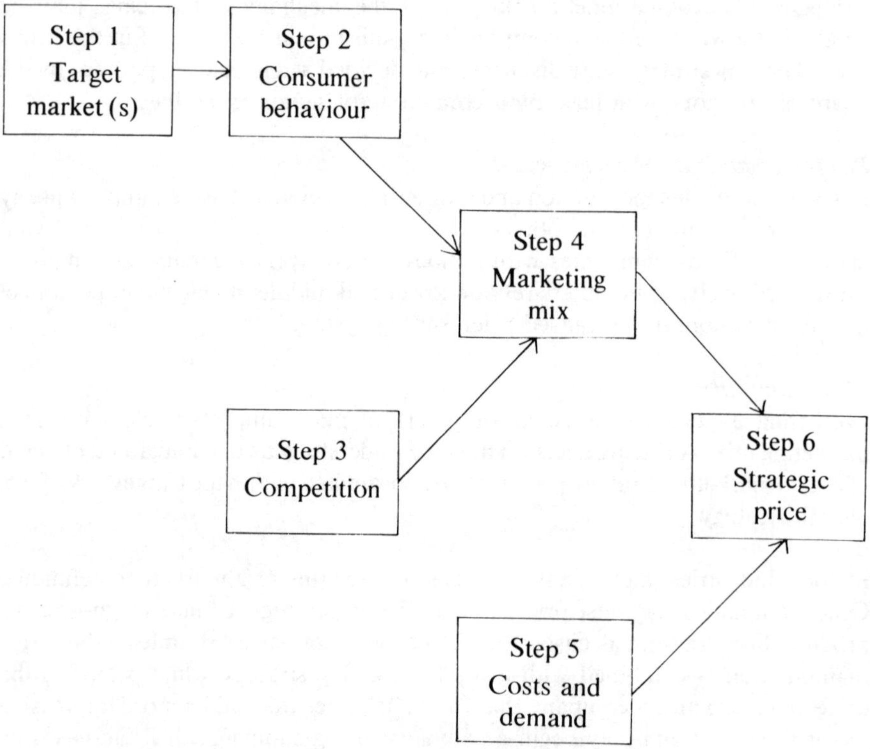

Figure 1 Strategic planning process

to market a new product and may examine what prices it can project for the product given the demand and competition in the market place. Afterwards, the company will determine an acceptable level of costs for producing the product and given its projections on prices, sales and profits.

4 Deciding on a strategy for pricing, given all the internal and external factors involved, is no easy matter. The larger an organisation is, the more it goes through the agonising process of weighing many variables in order to come to a pricing decision. The decision as to how to set up prices may look mechanistic, a simple matter of weighing all of the variables listed. While this might be ideally accomplished through a computer simulation, no such model is available. Figure 1 offers a concise model of the strategic pricing process. This kind of model can be useful to decision-makers, especially since it is designed to simplify each step so that the subsequent tasks of the next stage will appear more clear-cut.

The six steps in the process are:

(1) Select target market — this is perhaps the most fundamental marketing decision: what kinds of consumers will the firm pursue with its product? The company should decide on one or several market segments with promising sales potential.

(2) Study consumer behaviour — market research should be designed to present a picture of the target markets, their buying motives, location, sensitivity to price, prior attitudes about the marketer and the industry, and so on.

(3) Identify competition — the company should conduct an extensive investigation into its competitors in the industry, and also into other firms that may enter the industry in the future. What kinds of price, promotion, and other marketing strategies do they employ?

(4) Assign price role in the marketing mix — at this stage, the company desires estimates of the number of units that could be sold at various price levels. These estimates will be developed only after some thinking about non-price marketing strategies, for the company may want price estimates that conform to these non-price elements. Another task at this stage is to project the competitive reactions of other companies to each of the proposed pricing strategies.

(5) Relate costs and demand — costs will be estimated for producing a product at a number of levels of output. These levels will reflect projections for the demand for the product, which will be influenced by the price options in the earlier stage.

(6) Determine strategic price — the previous five stages set limits for the posssible price range of a product. At this point, marketing management will reflect on its overall objectives: satisfactory profits, share of the market, higher volume, ethical standards, and so on. It will then choose the price that best coincides with those objectives and the economic realities developed in the first five stages.

For this process to function effectively, the company has a critical need for accurate and complete information. Without this, an involved planning process will produce only an incorrect and possibly disastrous pricing strategy. Management must strive to develop the most efficient research and statistical techniques. Obviously, a key mistake at any one stage will throw the entire process out of line.

Pricing strategy is a most difficult challenge for marketers. Even so, marketers have little choice but to struggle to do their best. There is no retreat from the uncertainties of the strategic pricing process.

5 Market segmentation pricing, also known as price discrimination, is a form of demand-oriented pricing in which one product is given different prices depending on the segment of the market it is sold in. For example, vending machines normally command higher prices than supermarkets for chocolate bars, presumably because consumers are willing to pay a premium for the convenience or for the availability when other shops are closed.

The bases for market segmentation pricing are the customer, the product version, the place or the time:

(a) Customer segmentation is classically illustrated by the new car market. Two customers may buy identical cars from the same showroom, from the same salesman, on the same day, for different prices. The difference is the result of the customers' bargaining power; or from the car dealer's viewpoint he or she has managed to sell at a premium to one of the buyers.

(b) Price/version price differences occur when two slightly different products are sold for prices that differ by more than the cost of the product differences. Usually, the difference is largely psychological. The price difference between first class and economy on airlines is a good example.

(c) Place as a basis for price segmentation can be illustrated by the sometimes startling differences in cost between similar rooms at a hotel, depending on whether the view is of the lake or of the hotel's parking area.

(d) Time segmentation may take many forms, from seasonal price swings to cheap parking rates in the evening. On weekends, it costs more to fly, less to telephone. Theatre tickets are often priced lower for the matinée than for evening performances of the same show.

6 The problems in pricing new products are related to how different the product is from existing products already on the market. A new breakfast cereal or bath soap, for example, will be priced in line with the competitive products. A new product without close substitutes presents a different problem. In the past, such products were typically priced at cost plus a predetermined mark-up and then adjusted to anticipate competition. Now, many companies are taking advantage of the temporary monopoloy the product enjoys to set the market-oriented prices as high as a reasonable demand curve would seem to allow.

To set prices accurately for maximum profit, the company has to project potential demand, and the relation of price to sales. Consumer preferences must be established, and a range of prices set out that will make the product economically attractive to buyers. High initial prices may help to recoup development costs; low initial prices may help to keep competition at bay for a longer period. Both approaches are plausible depending on individual circumstances.

The basic decision, then, in pricing the new product is whether to go in with a high initial price, thus skimming the top of the market, or to start with low prices with the goal of market penetration.

Skimming strategy
With the introduction of every new or innovated product, there is a group of consumers who are willing to pay premium prices in order to be the first to try it. This provides a unique opportunity to launch the product at a high price and skim this lucrative top off the market before competition inevitably forces the prices down. This is, of course, not a high volume segment of the market; production, however, may not be at a high volume at this stage anyway. Skimming can help cover research development costs, hold sales figures down while design and production problems are solved, and create prestige for the product.

The objectives of skimming should be clearly laid out by the company: the lower the skimming price, the more visibility can be expected for the product from those who will not buy initially but who will be prospects once the price comes down. In other cases, the company may wish at first to limit production of a semi-experimental model by setting a high initial price.

Skimming works best when there is little chance of competitors entering the market quickly, especially when the product is protected by a patent. This advantage must be balanced against the incentive a high skimming price may give to competitors to speed up their plans for entry.

Skimming also succeeds among certain products with high visibility and prestige. The new wristwatch calculators, electric cars and home video recorders are some examples.

Penetration strategy
The penetration approach calls for a price low enough to get the product as deeply into the market as possible, establish brand loyalty and keep two steps ahead of the competition. Penetration may be instituted as a strategy at the time of the product launch or it may follow a skimming period.

Penetration pricing requires a carefully constructed programme, especially if it is part of a plan to reduce prices gradually. As initial costs begin to be paid off, either by skimming or initial sales volume, the unit cost goes down and many companies are tempted to base their selling price reductions on a cost plus basis. For full effectiveness, however, penetration strategy should take market demand into consideration. It is also wise to anticipate competitive pressure and stay ahead of it, rather than reduce prices in response to it.

The penetration approach in some ways requires more courage and commitment than skimming in that the break-even point is further down the line and therefore there is no promise of early profits. One danger of a penetration strategy is in setting the price so low that demand exceeds supply, thus hindering market penetration and allowing competitors time to catch up.

7 It is generally accepted that price flexibility is determined by the options in the price structure that raise or lower the price. It is also influenced by variations that occur through negotiations between buyer and seller. For example, widespread shortages of materials might force many marketers into more flexible sales contacts.

Most retailers today use what is known as a *single price policy*. This means that all buyers must pay the same price for the product, regardless of the quantity being purchased or any other market factors. For example, a student going to a university privately must pay a fixed fee for tuition each term, regardless of sex, race, ethnic background, income level, age, class standing or similar factors.

A *one-price policy* offers the same price to all customers who purchase the same quantity of goods under similar circumstances. But, unlike a single price policy, it allows for price to vary according to the quantity of the purchase. Many retailers favour a one-price policy because it is easy to administer. Also, it is equally fair to all buyers because it eliminates bargaining.

Under a policy of *varying prices,* different buyers purchasing the same quantity of a product under identical conditions may pay different prices. Competitive market factors, including the desire to make a sale, may lead to price reductions or increases. This type of policy is advantageous to sellers, since it allows for adjustments to meet prevailing market conditions. But varying prices often means that the pricing authority must be delegated to sales personnel in the field. This can be counter-productive, especially if a sales manager continually lowers prices in order to complete difficult transactions.

Price shading has become a dominant practice in some industries. Under this policy, list prices become little more than a starting point for negotiations with the salesman in the field. For example, an item may be purchased for 30% or more below the list price. Some companies have found these practices intolerable and have begun procedures to encourage or require the restriction of price shading.

Escalation clauses have become common in business deals. The buyer pays the going prices of labour, materials and production costs at the time of delivery, rather than at the time of order. On the surface this may seem a fair way for sellers to cover their costs in a time of inflation. But, as some manufacturers have noted: 'The price quoted to you when you placed the order no longer means a thing.' As a result some companies have discarded such clauses and now add surcharges to a fixed base price. This is designed to give the buyer a better idea of the likely increases.

8 Whether in terms of the initial pricing decision or the analysis of a price change, pricing has an element of strategy similar to a poker game. In pricing, as in poker, it is necessary to analyse the possible actions of all the players in the game.

Similarly, the company planning a price change must make extensive efforts to estimate the possible reactions of its competitors. In doing so, the company must decide whether any important competitor has a set 'price reaction' policy, or whether the competitor reacts differently to each unique situation. If the competitor has a set policy, it can be pinpointed through statistical analysis or through inside information. If a competitor has no set policy, it becomes important to analyse the competitor's financial situation and determine which objectives seem most important.

When a price reduction is initiated, a competitor's reactions are affected by a number of principal factors:

(a) *Costs* If costs are high, a competitor may not want to cut prices and reduce profits.

(b) *Speed* If a change in production methods is required to reduce costs and prices, it will probably take time.

(c) *Conflict of interests* If prices are cut, the competitor's 'quality line' and 'standard line' may be selling too close to each resulting in harm to both.

(d) *Relative sales volume* It is particularly costly for a large supplier to reduce prices to protect a certain segment of the market.

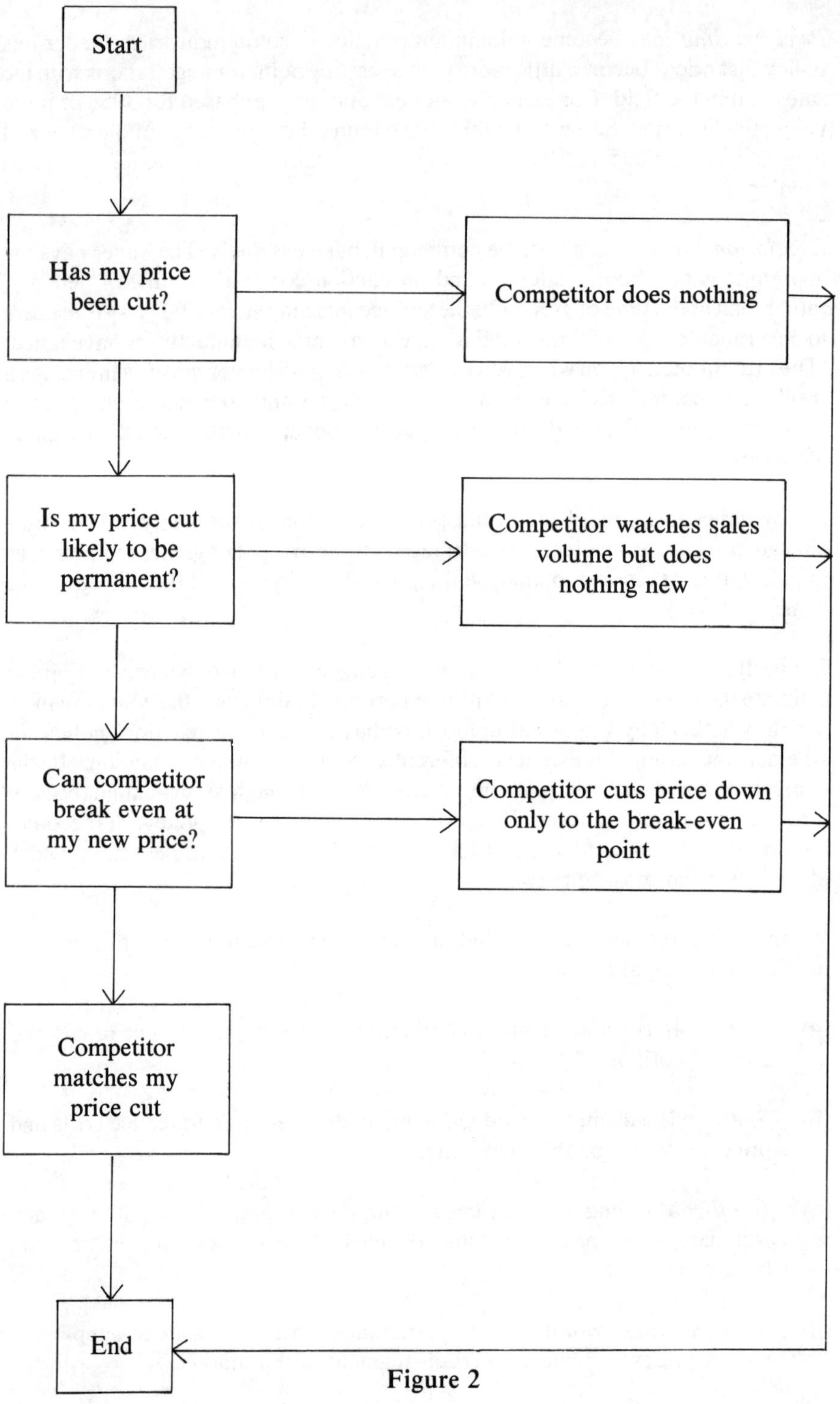
Start
Has my price been cut?
Competitor does nothing
Is my price cut likely to be permanent?
Competitor watches sales volume but does nothing new
Can competitor break even at my new price?
Competitor cuts price down only to the break-even point
Competitor matches my price cut
End

Figure 2

Figure 2 presents a logical flow model of competitor's reactions to a price cut. The model goes beyond the elementary question, 'Will he or won't he match my price cut?', to an examination of the more complex possibilities involved.

A price increase raises different sorts of problems in terms of evaluating competitor's reactions. In most situations the competitors will be asking three crucial questions:

(a) Will an industry-wide price increase reduce the total size of the market?

(b) How many other marketers are interested in following the initial rise?

(c) Has the initiator acted in the best interests of the industry as a whole?

9 *Promotion*

Very closely related to pricing is promotional strategy. An innovator must not only sell his product, but frequently he must also make people recognise their need for a new kind of product. The problem is one of 'creating a market'.

Initial promotion outlays are an investment in the product that cannot be recovered until some kind of market has been established. The innovator shoulders the burden of educating consumers to the existence and users of the product. Later imitators will never have to do this job; so if the innovator does not want to be simply a benefactor to his future competitors, he must make pricing plans to earn a return on all his initial outlays before his pricing discretion evaporates.

The basic strategic problem is to find the right mixture of price and promotion to maximise long-run profits. Relatively high prices may be chosen in the pioneering stages, together with large advertising and dealer discounts, and the plan may be to get the promotion investment back as soon as possible; or low prices and lean margins may be used from the very outset in order to discourage potential competition when the barriers of patents and investment in production capacity, distribution channels, or production techniques become inadequate.

Distribution

In respect of the relationship between distribution and price, choices of channels of distribution should be consistent with strategy for initial pricing and for initial outlay. Penetration pricing and explosive promotion call for distribution channels that promptly make the product broadly available. Otherwise advertising is wasted or mass market pricing is ruined. Distribution policy also concerns the role that the middleman plays in pushing a given product, the margins he must be paid to induce this action, and the amount of protection of territory and of inventory required to do it.

Estimation of the costs of moving the new product through the channels of distribution to the final consumer must enter into the pricing procedure, since these costs govern the factory price that will result in a specified final price. Distributive margins are partly pure promotional costs and partly physical distribution costs. Margins must at least cover the distributors' costs of warehousing, handling and administration. These costs are similar to factory production costs in being related to physical capacity and its utilisation i.e. fluctuations in production or sales volume. Hence these set a floor to trade and distribution discounts. But distributors usually also contribute promotional effort, in point of sale pushing, local advertising and display, when it is made worth their while. These pure promotional aspects are more optional.

Distributors' margins are best determined by a study of distributors' alternatives. This does not mean that the distributors' gross margins on a given product must be the same as those on a rival product. They should instead produce competitive rates of return on the distributors' investments in inventory, shelf-space and sales capacity.

10 To price a product in the later stages of its life cycle, it is important to be able to tell when a product is approaching maturity. When the new product is about to slip into the commodity category, it is sometimes desirable to reduce real prices promptly as soon as the symptoms of deterioration appear. Some of the symptoms of degeneration of competitive status towards the commodity level are:

(a) A weakening in brand preference — this may become obvious by a higher gross elasticity of demand among leading products, the leading brand not being able to continue demanding as much a price premium as initially without losing position.

(b) Narrowing physical variation among products as the best designs are developed and standardised — this has been dramatically demonstrated in the motor car industry and is still in process in television receivers.

(c) The entry in force of private label competitors — this is exemplified by the mail order houses sale of own-label refrigerators.

(d) Market saturation — the ratio of replacement sales to new equipment sales serves as an indicator of the competitive degeneration of durable goods, but in general it must be kept in mind that both market size and degree of saturation are hard to define.

(e) The stabilisation of production methods — this is indicated by a slow rate of technological advance, high average age of equipment, and great uniformity among competitors in production technology.

7 Selling

INTRODUCTION

This chapter covers the sales function and the role of selling in the marketing mix. This includes:

(a) The preparation for selling: setting salesforce objectives, prospecting for new customers, planning the sales presentation, measuring sales potential.

(b) Personal selling: obtaining the interview, sales presentations and techniques, demonstrations, sales aids, overcoming objectives and closing the sale.

(c) Sales responsibilities: relationships with customers, self-management, entertaining, report writing, information feedback and ethics.

QUESTIONS

1 Describe the different types of selling.

2 What are the basic steps in the personal selling process?

3 'The success of a sales programme depends largely on developing a high calibre salesforce.' Discuss how you would carry out this task.

4 How can you plan the organisational structure of the salesforce?

5 Describe the roles of the salesman.

6 Once customers have been identified, sales managers can develop strategies to guide the efforts of their salesforces. How would you do this?

7 How would you evaluate and control individual salesmen and sales operations?

8 What are the stages in the sales process?

9 What techniques can a salesman use to close a sale?

10 Describe and write up what you consider should be a comprehensive job description of a salesman, using any industry as an example.

ANSWERS

1 All personal sales jobs are not created the same. For this reason, several ways of classifying them have been established. One of the classifications identifies four basic types of selling: trade, missionary, technical, and new business.

Trade

Trade selling is done in many industries, particularly food, textiles, clothing, and wholesaling. These are areas where products are well established so that high-powered selling is not necessary.

The trade salesman's job is to build up volume by providing customers with promotional assistance. This type of salesman sells through, rather than to, customers. As a result, the trade saleman must understand how the customer runs his or her business. Being helpful and persuasive are more important than being aggressive, since the trade salesman must wear well with customers.

Missionary

Personal selling assistance is the key to stimulating more or seeking new sales. The medical salesman is a good example. He calls on physicians as the representative of a drug company, attempting to persuade them to prescribe the company's products for their patients' ailments.

Missionary salesmen, like trade salesmen, use a low key approach. They are, however, selling direct to customers, rather than through them. The successful missionary salesman is thoroughly familiar with the market, and can make an effective presentation of product benefits.

Technical

A technical salesman is like a professional consultant: he must be able to tell the customer what his buying needs are. The company will view such a salesman as a means of increasing sales volume to existing customers through additional product uses, especially in areas such as chemicals, machinery and heavy equipment. Since the technical salesman sells directly to the user or buyer, technical competence is as important as being personable.

New business

The new business salesman, as the name indicates, is concerned with obtaining new accounts. This process is also referred to as canvassing, or cold calling. A new business salesman has to be tough and able to withstand rejection. Because the demands are so great, the turnover rate in new business selling is very high.

2 The basic steps in the personal selling process must be totally mastered by every salesperson. In professional selling, the process may be carried out by a team of specialists and may take months or even years.

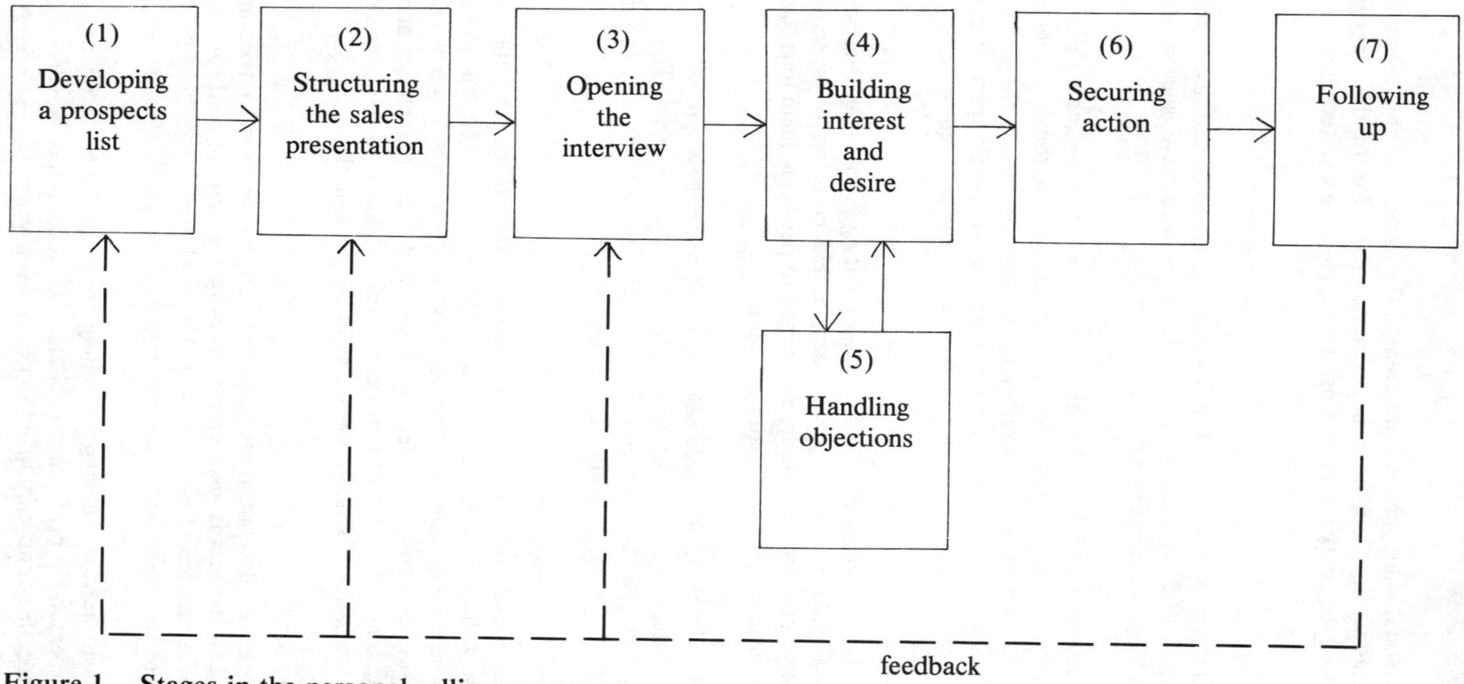

Figure 1 **Stages in the personal selling process**

The personal selling process is illustrated in Figure 1. The first step is to develop a list of prospects. Prospects include existing and potential customers who have a likely need for the product, and the ability to purchase it. In some companies this list is provided; in others the individual salesperson must develop contacts by scouting out leads.

The next step is to create a presentation. It can be completely unstructured, that is, the salesperson describes the product in any way he or she sees fit, or fully automated, accompanied by video film, slides or film strips, or it can fall anywhere in between. Generally, firms use several types of presentation simultaneously. The unstructured form is particularly popular, especially once a salesperson has gained experience and confidence.

The third step is to conduct an interview. The interview should generally go according to the 'AIDA theory'. Figure 2 briefly illustrates this theory. AIDA divides the buying process into four stages through which the buyer passes mentally: attention, interest, desire, action. Unless favourable attention is

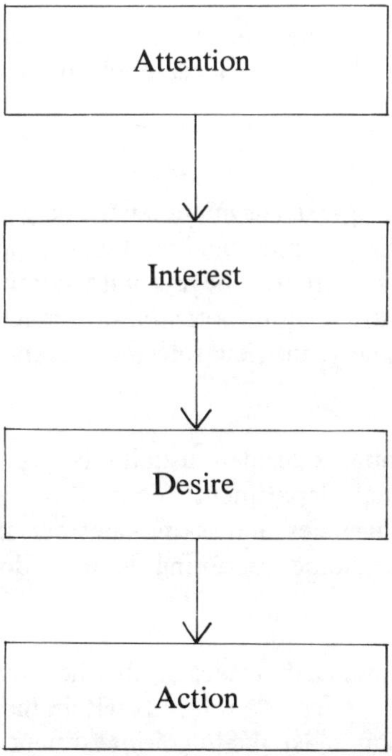

Figure 2

secured, the interview will not go much further. Next, the salesperson tries to arouse the buyer's interest and desire, often by exploring his or her needs and problems and how the product relates to them.

Handling objections is part of the salesperson's job during the interest and desire stage. It can rarely be assumed that the interview will go exactly as the salesperson wishes. In reality, the customer often raises objections. He may want more time to think, may question the product's value, dislike the terms of sale, or indicate a lack of confidence in the salesperson. The ability to face objections is acquired with time and experience.

The climax of the sales presentation is the securing of action. The sale may be closed with the customer's decision to buy or not to buy, or a meeting may be scheduled with other personnel who influence the buying position. The customer may be ready to say 'yes' early in the interview or not until much time and talk have passed.

The successful salesperson does not let the matter end with the close of a sale. Following up is an important part of the selling process. It includes checking on how well the product is selling for a retail customer, or how satisfied the retail customer is.

3 It is certainly a fact that the sales programme does depend on developing a high calibre salesforce. Such a salesforce could be developed in the following ways.

Proper staffing is crucial
Although the selection of good salesmen cannot be guaranteed, management's aim is to find people with potential that can be developed through training and motivation. The selection process begins with careful job analysis and job description. It proceeds to recruiting potential salesmen by choosing from among available candidates. Finally, the new salesmen receive some type of training.

Recruiting
The selection of potential salesmen usually begins with recruiting efforts. Typically, the personnel department recruits by placing advertisements, contacting employment agencies, and asking salesmen already with the company to suggest possibilities. Some recruiting is also done at universities and colleges.

A typical national sales manager suggested that he would 'contact employment agencies, professional societies, use referrals within the industry. We just could not afford to take any man, make the major investment for two or three years in him, and then have him selling the training we gave him to somebody else'. Good companies are therefore looking for salesmen who can become productive immediately. Sales quotas are so large and selling costs so high that a company cannot afford non-productive employees.

Selection

Many criteria dictate the selection of a salesforce. Does the organisation want experienced professionals or qualified trainees? Training is expensive, and it may be more economical to select people who already know the job. If very specialised experience is being sought, however, the search may prove difficult and costly.

In general, companies are concerned with the individual's health, physical appearance, verbal fluency and adaptability. Many companies routinely give psychological screening tests. These tests are useful in identifying traits of character and personality, but they cannot be used as the sole criterion. Other companies develop lists of qualities deemed important to the good salesman. But such lists are static: they cannot be used to predict how the salesman will interact with customers in a dynamic situation.

Training

The training process is most effective when there is interaction between the salesman and the instructor. It is influenced by individual attitudes, the goals of the training, and methods of teaching and evaluation.

Training can range from on-the-job training to formal classroom sessions. On-the-job training means the salesman actually learns by doing the new job under the supervision of a seasoned salesman or sales manager. This approach is attractive because it is cheaper and faster. But it runs the risk of producing graduates little more than imitators of people with relatively narrow experience.

There are several methods for off-the-job training. Choice will depend on specific objectives as well as the content of the training.

(a) The case method — trainees are asked to discuss problem situations in a classroom setting. The situations are usually selling encounters with difficult customers.

(b) Role-play — the trainee acts out a problem in order to experience it emotionally. This experience is used to test insights into the problem.

(c) The T-group method — trainees interact with each other whilst discussing specific topics. The aim is to increase understanding of how people interact with each other.

(d) Operational gaming — a computerised or manually operated model of a hypothetical organisation allows the trainee to use decision-making capabilities. Certain questions are answered about selling strategics and tactics. Rapid feedback reports the results of decisions.

Deciding which training approach is best means analysing objectives. If memorisation of technical information is the goal, written tests will probably serve the purpose. Whatever method is used, the test of value is subsequent performance. A student may do well in training, but the real test is his or her ability to interact and communicate in the actual selling encounter.

4 In planning an organisation for the salesforce, management should take many things into consideration. These include the size of the company, the nature of the market and of product lines, and the types of personnel in the organisation. No single organisation structure is suited to all salesforces. In one company, management may decide that all sales people should sell all products. In another, it may be more practical to have individuals assigned to a single product.

Size

What is the right size for the salesforce? Some analysts have worked out a system based on equalising work load. The method assumes that management has determined the economical number of calls to make on accounts of different sizes. Using this formula, a company may estimate that there are 1,000 major accounts and 2,000 less major accounts in the entire country. The major accounts require 36 calls a year, and the secondary accounts 12 calls. The company then needs a salesforce that can make 60,000 sales calls per year. If the average salesman can make 1,000 calls per year, the company needs 60 full-time salesmen.

Some managers have the mistaken impression that the number of salesmen should be determined by the number of sales, rather than the other way round. These managers are likely to add to the salesforce when sterling sales are up and to fire them when sterling sales are down. But this represents a distorted view of the salesman's role. The salesman is the one who brings about new sales, and adding to the force is a capital investment. The managers should compare the expected rate of return with the expected rate of other corporate investments before deciding to hire or to fire salesmen.

Design

The effectiveness of the salesforce depends primarily on how it is organised. Various types of design structure are possible; the following are a few of the most popular:

(a) Territories — under the simplest sales structure, each salesman represents the company's full product range in a specific territory. Such an organisation defines the salesman's responsibilities clearly, as failure in sales in the area must be laid directly on his shoulders. This structure encourages the salesman to develop personal and business ties in the area. Such a structure also reduces travel expenses.

(b) Products — many companies find that assigning the salesforce according to product line has advantages, especially when the products are technically complex, highly unrelated or very numerous. But just because a company offers different products does not mean that a product-structured salesforce is necessary. If one customer buys many separate product lines, for example, the set-up can be a disadvantage. Company salesmen may be treading on each other's toes, and lining up to see the same customers.

(c) Customers — a customer-structured salesforce has a major advantage in that it allows sales personnel to be more thoroughly aware of the customer's needs. There are several ways of structuring a salesforce by customer. These include breakdown by size, nature of business, and methods of distribution. But like the product-oriented structure, a customer-oriented set-up has disadvantages of overlapping coverage of sales territories.

The National Cash Register Company is an example of a very large company that sells by industry rather than by product lines.

(d) Key accounts — with increasing frequency sales efforts are being organised on the basis of major accounts. Usually, a major buyer has a number of units whose purchases are directed by a central corporate group, although individual branches may make the actual purchases.

(e) Other variations — some companies have developed still other variations on sales organisations. At IBM salesmen specialise by function, including maintenance and upgrading of systems, equipment protection and installation. Other companies organise on a sequential basis: executives isolate the separate markets for each product line and focus on a single market before moving on to the next.

5 The major role of a salesman is, of course, to sell the company's product line. But other responsibilities may be even more important than selling. These are:

Determining customer needs

When approaching a new customer the salesman has a first task — to listen. The salesman should then help the customer to find his or her combination of products and specifications to satisfy needs, even if it means recommending competitive products. The role of the salesman is as a consultant, that is, an expert interested in solving the customer's problems, in winning greater acceptance, particularly in industrial sales.

Prospecting

Salesmen must try to identify potential buyers as well as to service existing buyers. The natural inclination is to rely on existing accounts to increase sales. This is a less risky means of gaining commission than prospecting for new accounts. Yet prospecting is the only way to ensure future sales and profitability.

Providing marketing intelligence
Salesmen must report changes in needs, buyer behaviour, and competitive activity to their sales managers. They should also be encouraged to make recommendations regarding product design and additions to or deletions from the product range based on the feedback of information from buyers.

Communicating information to buyers
Salesmen must communicate information to buyers on company capabilities including product lines, product specifications, price, delivery, and service.

Providing service
Each customer buys three things: the product and what it will do, the reputation of the manufacturer, and the treatment and service provided by the salesman. Often service outweighs other factors in gaining sales. In many product categories, specification and price are fairly standard. Good salesmen must then concentrate on factors that could differentiate his company from others — technical assistance, financing, delivery, post-purchase service.

Implementing trade or consumer promotions
In many consumer goods companies, the salesman's primary task is to get wholesalers and retailers to use company promotions. This activity, merchandising, is the first line salesman's primary responsibility in such companies as Procter and Gamble, Marlboro, Unilever. When a sales representative of one of these major companies goes into a supermarket chain, he does not have to sell the product. These are leading brands that are stocked by most stores. The salesman is serving only as an order-taker for these items. The creative task is to use the company's displays, to run a price promotion, or to get the brand stocked prominently in the store.

Supporting advertising
Salesmen should also support the other component of the promotional mix, advertising. The sales approach should be consistent with the advertising appeals. Salesmen who refer to the advertising reinforce its message, having more of an effect on the buyer. Many marketers believe that an educated salesforce can give an advertising programme an extra 20% in effectiveness. Industrial salesmen are particularly reliant on advertising. They view industrial aids such as advertising as a calling card for new accounts.

6 Sales strategies can vary according to the salesman's approach to the customer. Salesmen can approach customers by trying to emphasise their expertise, or by trying to establish empathy and to emphasise their similarity to the customer. If the salesman is trying to establish expertise, he should take a more informational approach by communicating product specifications and capabilities. A salesman taking an empathetic approach should establish rapport and friendship while delivering the sales message. After examining the literature and conducting several studies, a researcher concluded that expertise should be established if:

(a) the salesman has the product knowledge and credentials for legitimately seeking to be seen as an expert;

(b) the customer is engaged in a high risk, complex buying task that requires expertise; and

(c) the salesman does not regularly sell to the buyer, creating more of a need to establish his or her credentials.

Sales strategies can also vary depending on whether the salesman is trying to reinforce existing customers needs and beliefs, or trying to change them. These alternatives, expertise versus empathy and reinforcement versus change, combine to produce the selling strategies illustrated in the table below.

Approach to customers needs and beliefs	Approach to customers	
	Emphasise knowledge and expertise	Emphasise empathy
Reinforce needs and/or beliefs	Identify and meet existing needs	Demonstrate similarity to customer
Change needs and/or beliefs	Change: ● Beliefs about products ● Consumer needs Provide: Information on: * New products * New features	Change: Customer perceptions of buyer-seller interaction

Personal selling strategies

Strategies emphasising expertise
If the salesman decides to emphasise expertise in meeting existing needs he must identify and meet those needs. If the salesman decides that a change strategy would best fill customer needs, he can attempt to change beliefs about existing products, change needs, or provide information on new brands or new features of existing brands.

Strategies emphasising empathy
If a salesman decides to emphasise empathy in an impersonal context, the best approach to meeting existing needs is to establish his or her similarity to the customer. Personal relations are then established on the customer's perception of empathy, and the salesman can then proceed to determine how to best meet customer needs from the company's product line. A changed strategy would be required if the salesman felt that the proper interpersonal relationship had not been established to make a sale. A salesman would then attempt to change the customer's perceptions to establish similarity and empathy.

7 The sales manager has the dual responsibility of evaluating the overall sales effort and the efforts of individual salesmen. The criteria used to evaluate a salesman's performance vary widely. One survey of industrial companies found that sales volume was the most widely used criterion. A more effective measure is, of course, the relation of sales volume to sales quota to determine if the salesman has fulfilled the potential in his territory.

The weakness of volume and quota criteria is that they may not be related to profitability. Sales quotas might have been achieved at excessive cost. A more effective measure of performance would be to determine the salesman's contribution to profits. Another survey of industrial companies found that whereas two-thirds of the companies interviewed used sales-volume criteria, only about one-quarter used profit criteria. Perhaps some companies have inadequate records to determine the contribution to a particular salesman makes to profits by product and territory.

Profitability measures should be used with other criteria in evaluating a sales performance. The following criteria could be used in evaluating the salesman's allocation of time and fulfilment of administrative assignments:

(a) the number of calls per customer;
(b) expenses per sales call;
(c) number of new customers obtained;
(d) number of customers lost;
(e) the completion of sales call reports; and
(f) fulfilment of post-purchase service and maintenance requirements.

The sales manager's primary concern in the area of control is expenses, particularly in travel and entertainment. These expenses must be controlled to maximise profitability. A second area of control is the salesman's time. I have heard of a sales executive who estimates that the average salesman spends a quarter of the time selling, another quarter doing administration work, and half of the time travelling, waiting, or servicing customers. Because so much time is spent on tasks that do not generate revenue, the sales manager must try to develop more effective allocation of the salesman's time.

A third area of control is ensuring that salesmen fulfil necessary administrative tasks by making out daily and weekly reports and developing lists of prospective new customers.

8 One of the best ways of answering this question is to use a model such as that shown in Figure 3, which describes a customer-oriented sales process. In the first step the salesman combines past knowledge of the customer with specific information gained from the current contact to form an impression of the needs of the customer. Using this impression, the salesman formulates a strategy. The strategy can be based on meeting or changing customer needs or attitudes. As in advertising, a changed strategy is more difficult to implement. Such a strategy might require that the salesman attempt to change customer beliefs about a product or the priority of customer needs. As an example of the sales process, a salesman for a producer of forklift trucks visits a regular customer and determines that the customer's priorities have changed. The customer is not as concerned with the price. More emphasis is being placed on heavier loads and greater mobility. Both the salesman and the customer know that the two needs are not entirely compatible. Greater load weight means more limited mobility. Therefore, the salesman's strategy is to educate the customer on the various trade-offs that can be achieved between load weight and mobility. He formulates a message to educate the customer but without alienating him. In so doing, he tries to communicate the company's options in terms of these two criteria.

In the third step the salesman transmits the message and waits for the reaction from the customer. The customer expresses interest in several heavy duty models that do not really satisfy mobility requirements. On further questioning, the customer admits that the mobility is not as important a criterion as load weight. There is no need for the salesman to adjust sales strategy as the buyer is a long-standing customer, and takes no offence at his educational approach. Further feedback establishes price level, delivery requirements, and service needs.

The result of this type of interaction is not necessarily a sale; it may be that the buyer decides to look into several competitive lines. But the salesman's objectives have been met, since he has established the options that his company can offer and the terms of sale. Furthermore, because the buyer perceives the salesman as customer-oriented and views the company as a reliable and quality-oriented manufacturer, the salesman knows that the chances of closing the sale are high.

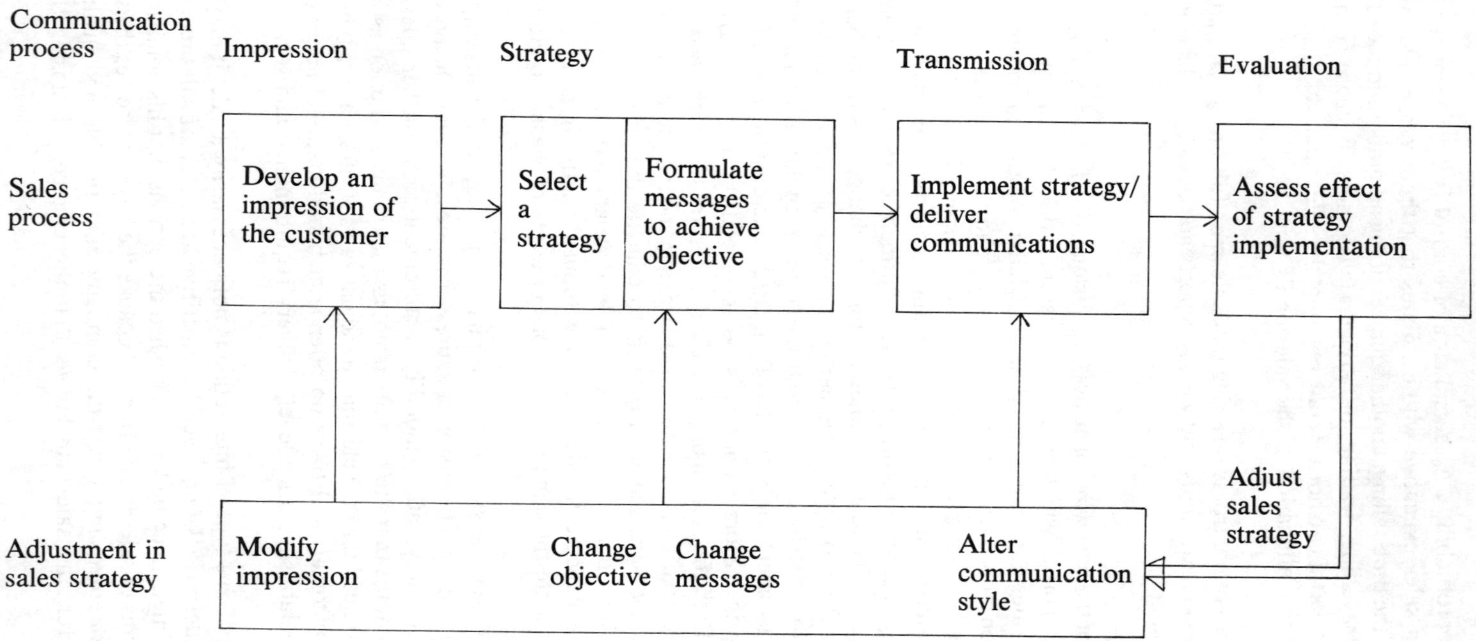

Figure 3 The sales process

Figure 3 shows that the salesman must evaluate the customer's response to the sales process at each step and make the proper adjustment. Because of what the customer says, the salesman might modify his impressions of the customer, change the objectives of the sales presentation, change the message being transmitted, or alter the way the sales message is being presented.

This model is not just a model of the sales process, but it is also a communications process, since personal selling is communication.

9 Salesmen often feel that a good approach, effective presentation and a skilful handling of objections should suffice to achieve the desired results. Many fail to realise that an individual nudge, a direct effort, is necessary to make it easier for the buyer to decide. Closing techniques are, in effect, the final thrust that help the almost fully persuaded buyer to act favourably towards the salesman. There are basically four closing techniques, the employment of which will depend upon the circumstances in a specific situation.

(a) *The assumptive technique* This is used when the salesman has encountered little resistance from the buyer. The salesman merely assumes agreement. For example, a salesman selling coffee to the institutional market has as his objective on one call to get the manager of the restaurant to agree to sample a new, richer blend. He receives few objections during the presentation and the manager appears to be interested. Sensing the situation, the salesman says, 'I'll add a 5 lb can of the new blend to your regular order, and I'll be back next week to get your reaction.'

(b) *The choice technique* This technique is usually employed when the salesman encounters some resistance. It makes use of at least two positive alternatives. It gives the buyer a choice between something and something. For example, a freight salesman for an airline calling on a cargo manager who has raised a number of objections at the point of closing should not say, 'On which flight shall I put the shipment?', but should rather say, 'Would you prefer to get the shipment on the 8 o'clock flight or the midnight flight?'

(c) *The summary technique* When the presentation is lengthy, and involves many complex features and relies on more than one benefit, the summary technique is desirable. An encapsulated review of the highlights which have stimulated the most positive responses should help to induce favourable action. This technique is best combined with the choice technique.

(d) *Special feature technique* There are occasions when a unique event or a special situation will be used as a basis for closing. The special feature technique is employed when unusual conditions such as supply shortage, a strike, or an increase in price is anticipated. The technique is used under exceptional circumstances by the professional salesman, and then only when all the information is thoroughly validated.

10 A typical job description should describe the salesman's job and should also specify the territory to be covered.

The job description should contain the following:

(a) the job title;
(b) a statement of the basic objective of the job;
(c) a description of the line organisation or relationship;
(d) an enumeration of the functional relationship;
(e) details of the specific responsibilities the salesman must carry out to perform his job satisfactorily.

Job title
In the example, the title is merely salesman. It might also be account representative, sales engineer, or some other selling title.

Basic objective
This statement should be succinct, and generally limited to a short paragraph in which the basic responsibility of the salesman is emphasised in a very forthright manner.

Line relationship
It is also necesary to name the salesman's superior. Hopefully this is a single relationship.

Functional relationships
Although the salesman should have a single line relationship, he may also be asked to carry out special duties on behalf of managers or staff departments to whom, during the course of a project, he will have a functional relationship. He may also have relatively permanent responsibilities to report certain information to staff departments. In any case, these relationships should be described in this section of the description as, for example, reports pertaining to market research data for the director of market research.

Specific responsibilities
This section should cover the details of actually carrying out the sales job, such matters as account schedules, expenses, regular reporting requirements and required administrative work.

Below is an example of a typical job description.

Job description

Position title: SALESMAN

The basic objective of the job
To represent the ABC Company in the territory described in the agreement by maintaining excellent relations with current ABC customers and by seeking to increase the number of such customers. He will be sensitive to special customer situations that may call for special treatment. He will be alert to all events and situations that effect the success of the ABC Company in maintaining and improving its position as a supplier of its product to companies in the territory.

Line relationship
Reports to the regional sales manager.

Functional relationships
Represent the credit control manager on request.
Report market intelligence to the director of market research.
Report competitive price developments to the pricing manager.

Specific responsibilities
It is expected that a salesman will:

(a) Average at least five sales calls per day.

(b) Whenever possible, encourage customers to place their orders directly by telephone.

(c) Keep his transport and other expenses to a minimum, and in any case seek prior approval for entertainment expenses in excess of £20 per week.

(d) Keep the sales office informed of his whereabouts at all times by filing daily and weekly itineries.

(e) Submit each week detailed time sheets in the form prescribed by the company; submit orders and other sales documents in the form prescribed by the company; and keep the procedures section of his sales manual up-to-date by filing additions and replacement pages within one day after their receipt.

8 Advertising and sales promotion

INTRODUCTION

This chapter covers the areas of advertising and sales promotion. It includes: communicating unique selling propositions and availability of products and services; converting of consumer needs into effective demand; support for the sales force; specialised agencies; point of sale promotions; merchandising; the advertising promotion mix; public relations; and the role of conferences and exhibitions.

QUESTIONS

1 'The promotion mix is a combination of advertising, publicity, personal selling, and/or sales promotion.' Explain.

2 What factors would the marketing management need to take into consideration when selecting appropriate media?

3 What is cooperative advertising?

4 Explain how you would establish an advertising plan and illustrate typical advertising objectives.

5 In advertising and promotion, what is meant by feedback?

6 How would you measure the results of advertising?

7 'In advertising, the presentation of a message involves careful evaluation of the message and its form.' Explain.

8 How would you establish advertising objectives?

9 What factors would you consider in allocating an advertising budget?

10 Two of the many differences between industrial and consumer advertising are:

(a) industrial advertising tends to support personal selling; and
(b) it is a less important part of the promotional mix.

Discuss.

ANSWERS

1 After establishing a total promotion budget, the company must determine its promotion mix. The promotion mix is the overall and specific communication programme of the company, consisting of the combination of advertising, publicity, personal selling and/or sales promotion.

It is rare for a company to use only one type of promotion; for example, a mail order company relying on advertising, a hospital totally on publicity, or a local market vendor on personal selling. In most cases a mix of promotional types is used. For example, the large group, General Foods, has a salesforce that visits every supermarket in which its products are stocked; it advertises in newspapers and magazines and on television, and distributes sales promotional price-cut coupons. The multi-national IBM has a large technical salesforce, advertises heavily in business and trade publications, and sends representatives to trade shows.

It is important to remember that each type of promotion serves a different function, and therefore complements the other types. Advertisements appeal to large audiences and create awareness; without them, the personal sales effort is much more difficult, time-consuming and expensive. Publicity provides credible information to a wide audience, but its content and timing cannot be controlled by the company. Personal selling offers one-to-one contact, flexibility, and the ability to close sales; without it, the initial interest caused by advertisements would be wasted. Sales promotions stimulate short-run sales and supplement advertising and selling.

The promotion mix varies by type of company. A small company is restricted in the kind of advertisements it can afford or use efficiently. It would emphasise personal selling. A large company covers a sizeable geographical area and would stress advertising as well as personal selling. A non-profit company would seek as much publicity as possible. A consumer company would feature the advertising of its brands; but an industrial company would count on a major personal selling effort.

In general, the following factors should be considered when developing a promotion mix.

Consumers
A large, dispersed target market favours advertising; a small, concentrated market favours personal selling. Organisational consumers require more personal attention than final consumers. Distribution channel members are often asked for promotional support. Some consumers are more persuadable than others. Some react poorly to personal selling and prefer self-service. Media use can be determined through demographic profiles.

Budget
A limited budget eliminates advertising on television or in magazines and directs efforts at personal selling and local newspapers. A large budget allows full use of all tools possible. After the budget is set, its degree of percentage allocation by promotion type is then needed.

Products
Highly technical and complex products and expensive items require a greater level of personal selling than simple, inexpensive items which depend upon advertising. As products move through the life cycle, message content and the promotional mix change. Initial emphasis is on information and the creation of primary demand. Then persuasion is used and selective demand generated. Finally, reminder messages are used to sustain demand. Products that are difficult to differentiate from the competition require more personal selling than those with distinct differential advantages.

Competition
Each company establishes its own long-run promotion mix, after examining the competition, based on its particular needs. Companies frequently match short-run advertising expenditures or special promotions of competitors.

Media
The media that are available to the company must be determined. Some media require the placement of advertisements well in advance of their appearance, others need a short lead time.

Place of purchase
Distribution through discount stores or direct mail means extensive advertising and self-service purchases. Sales through full service stores combine advertising *and* personal selling.

2 Marketing management has a wide variety of media from which to choose. When selecting media, these factors should be considered:

(a) cost;
(b) waste;
(c) reach;
(d) frequency;
(e) message permanence;
(f) persuasive impact;
(g) clutter; and
(h) lead time.

Advertising costs should be assessed in two ways. First, the total costs of a medium are calculated; for example, £20,000 for a full-page colour advertisement in a national magazine. Second, per reader or viewer costs are computed. Costs are expressed on a per thousand basis, except by some large newspapers which use a cost per million base. If the £20,000 advertisement is placed in a magazine with a circulation of 500,000, the cost per thousand can easily be calculated.

Waste is the portion of the audience that is not in the target market. Because media appeal to mass audiences, waste is a significant factor in advertising. This can be demonstrated with a continuation of the magazine illustration above. The publication might well be a special interest magazine for amateur photographers. Through marketing research, the company knows that 450,000 readers will have an interest in a new fast speed film; but 50,000 have no interest in the film, representing the wasted audience for an advertisement on fast speed film.

Reach refers to the number of viewers or readers in the audience. For television and radio, reach is the total number of people who are exposed to an advertisement. For print media, reach has two components; circulation and passing over rate. Circulation is the number of copies sold and distributed to consumers. Passing over rate is the number of times each copy is placed with somebody else to read. For example, each copy of *Newsweek* magazine is read by about six people. The pass over rate for magazines is much higher than for daily newspapers.

Frequency is how often a medium can be used. It is greatest for newspapers, radio and television, where advertisements may appear daily and advertising strategy may be easily changed. Telephone directories, outdoor advertisements, and magazines have the poorest frequency. A yellow pages advertisement may be placed or changed only once per year.

Message permanence refers to the number of exposures one advertisement generates and how long it remains with the audience. Outdoor advertisements and telephone directories yield many exposures per message. In addition, magazines are retained by consumers for long periods of time. On the other hand, radio and television advertisements last only five, fifteen or thirty seconds and are over.

Persuasive impact is the ability of a medium to stimulate consumers. Television often has the highest persuasive impact, particularly with high-volume consumer products, because it is able to combine audio, video, colour animation, and other appeal. Magazines also have a high persuasive impact. Many newspapers are improving their technology in order to feature full colour advertisements and increase their persuasive impact.

Clutter involves the number of advertisements that are contained in a single programme or issue of a medium. Clutter is low when a limited number of advertisements is presented, such as a company placing a few scattered commercials on television specials. Clutter is high when many advertisements are presented, such as the large number of supermarket advertisements that appear on a Friday in most of the weekly newspapers. Increasingly, television networks are being criticised for permitting too much clutter, particularly in allowing companies to sponsor very brief commercials.

Lead time is the time required by the medium for placing an advertisement. It is shortest for newspapers, and longest for magazines and telephone directories. A long lead time means that a firm must plan its advertising programmes six months or more in advance, and risk incorrect messages in a changing environment. Television may also require a long lead time because the number of advertisements it can carry is limited.

In recent years, there have been many media innovations. These include regional editions, local editions related to postal code areas to revive magazines; newspapers improving their computer skills in placing advertisements; advertising on cable television; televised commercials in supermarkets, cinemas, aeroplanes; specialised yellow pages; more radio stations handling advertisements in stereo; and better quality in outdoor signs.

3 In order to stimulate middlemen, and expand advertising efforts, the company should consider cooperative efforts. Under a cooperative advertising plan, middlemen members share the costs of some aspects of advertising. In a vertical cooperative advertising agreement, the channel members at different stages share costs. With a horizontal cooperative advertising agreement, two or more channel members at the same stage share costs, for example, two retailers.

Good cooperative agreements state the share of costs to be paid by each party, functions and responsibilities of each party, advertisements to be covered and the basis for termination.

The amount of cooperative advertising has increased tremendously since 1983. However, retailers used a very small percentage of the total amount spent. The non-use of cooperative advertising by many retailers was due to their perceptions of manufacturers' inflexibility involving messages and media, the costs of cooperative advertising to retailers, restrictive provisions, and the emphasis on the manufacturer's name in advertising. To remedy this, a number of manufacturers are now more flexible in the message or media they will support, paying for a large percentage of advertising cost, easing restrictive provisions, and featuring retailers' names more prominently in advertisements.

One example is Levi Strauss, who allow retailers to receive cooperative advertising money for messages placed in magazines, outdoor advertisements, statements enclosed with monthly bills sent to their credit account customers, local newspapers, and many other media. Previously, Levi was very strict about the media it would sponsor.

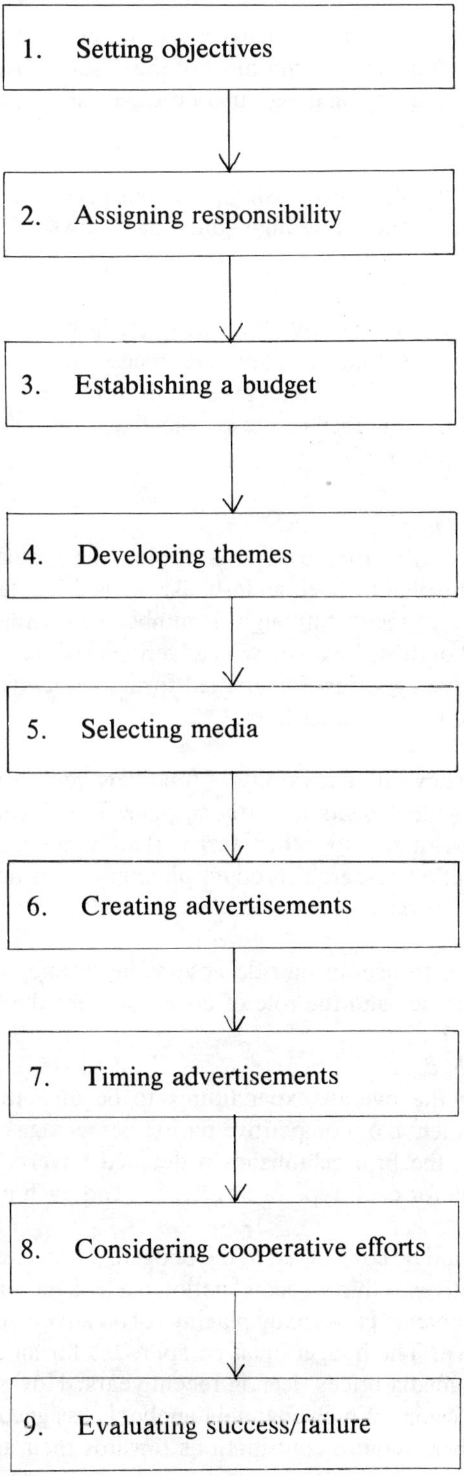

Figure 1 Development of an advertising plan

American Express participate in plans involving both vertical and horizontal cooperative advertising. They cover most of the costs of display advertisements emphasising their company; and a group of retailers share the remaining cost for listing their names in these advertisements.

4 The development of an advertising plan consists of the nine steps shown in Figure 1. These steps should be highlighted as follows.

Setting objectives

The advertising objectives set by a company guide its entire advertising plan. Objectives can be divided into demand and image types. The table below gives examples of several specific objectives a firm might set in each of those categories. Usually, a number of these objectives are combined and pursued through the advertising plan.

Assigning responsibility

In assigning responsibility for the advertising plan, the company has two options. It can undertake the plan through an in-house advertising department or hire an outside advertising agency. Although a number of companies have in-house departments, most of those involved with advertising on a sizeable or continuous basis employ outside agencies. Diversified firms frequently employ a different agency for each of their product lines.

An advertising agency offers a variety of functions, and usually works with the firm in the development of its advertising plan. This includes themes, media selection, copy writing, and other tasks. The large agencies offer a full complement of market research, product planning, consumer research, public relations and other services.

The firm's decision to use an outside advertising agency depends on its own expertise and resources and the role of advertising for the firm.

Establishing the budget

After determining the overall expenditures to be allocated by what can be afforded (by incremental or competitive parity, percentage of sales, or objective and task method), the firm establishes a detailed advertising budget. It must delineate the funds for each type of advertising and each medium.

Several points should be considered in the budgeting process. What are the costs of different alternatives, a thirty-second national television spot versus a full-page magazine advertisement? How many placings of an advertisement are necessary for it to be effective? The budget must be approved for an adequate number of places. How have media prices risen in recent years? How should the company react during a recession? Which channel member is assigned promotional tasks? Do channel members require contributions towards their advertising?

Type of objective	Illustrations
Demand-oriented	
Information	Create brand awareness of a new product by the target market. Explain the characteristics of a new product or service. Acquaint consumers with new opening hours. Reduce the time it takes for sales people to answer basic questions. Expand the existing base of customers by appealing to new geographic areas or market segments.
Persuasion	Improve brand ratings. Gain brand preference. Increase store traffic. Increase sales. Achieve brand loyalty.
Reminding (retention)	Stabilise sales. Maintain brand loyalty. Sustain brand recognition and image. Reinforce customer's brand preferences.
Image-oriented	
Industry	Develop and maintain a favourable industry image. Generate primary demand for products or services.
Company	Develop and maintain a favourable company image. Generate selective demand for products or services.

Developing themes
Next, a company develops advertising themes, the overall appeals for its campaign. A product or service appeal centres on the item and its attributes. Consumer appeal describes the product or service in terms of consumer benefits rather than product or service characteristics. A non-consumer, non-product or non-service appeal deals with institutional advertising and corporate image.

Selecting media
A company has a wide variety of media from which to choose. It should consider such factors as: cost, reach, message permanence, frequency, waste, clutter, lead time and persuasive impact.

Creating advertisements
Creating advertisements involves four fundamental decisions:

(a) The message content must be determined.
(b) A product schedule must be outlined.
(c) The firm needs to determine how many variations on its basic message to utilise.
(d) The location of an advertisement in a broadcast programme or print medium must be determined.

Timing advertisements
This requires two major decisions: how often a particular advertisement is shown, and when to advertise during the year. In the first decision the company must balance audience awareness and knowledge versus irritation if it places an advertisement a number of times in a short period of time. For example, McDonald's runs its advertisement repeatedly, but changes them very often.

Secondly, the company determines whether to advertise through the year or in concentrated periods.

Considering cooperative methods
Under a cooperative advertising plan, channel members share the costs of some aspects of advertising. In a vertical cooperative advertising agreement, channel members at different stages share costs, for example, manufacturer and retailer. With a horizontal cooperative advertising agreement, two or more channel members at the same stage share the costs, for example, two retailers.

Evaluating success/failure
The basic principles of evaluation and measuring the effectiveness of advertising are as follows:

(a) A good testing system examines data that are relevant to the objectives of the advertising under consideration.

(b) A good test system requires agreement about how results will be used before the analysis is conducted.

(c) A combination of measurement methods is desirable, because single methods are generally inadequate.

(d) A good testing system is based on the consumer's decision process, particularly reception of a stimulus, comprehension of the message, and behaviour response.

(e) The use of repetitious advertising is studied in a good testing system.

(f) When comparing alternative messages, each requires the same degree of support.

(g) Biases are to be avoided.

(h) Audience sampling is to be carefully specified.

(i) Good tests are valid and can be repeated with similar results.

5 Feedback is the response an audience makes to a company's message. It may take one of three forms: purchase, attitude change, or non-purchase. The company must understand that each of these three alternative responses is possible and develop the procedure for monitoring them.

The most desirable kind of feedback occurs when a consumer purchases a product or service after communications with or from the company. This means that the message is effective enough to stimulate a transaction.

The second type of feedback takes place when the company determines that its promotional efforts have elicited a favourable attitude change toward the company or its offerings by the audience. For new products or services, favourable attitudes must be created prior to consumer purchases: awareness — favourable attitude — purchase. For existing products, consumers may have bought a competing brand before the message was received or be temporarily out of money. The generation of favourable attitudes in these consumers may lead to future purchases.

The least desirable feedback neither purchases an item nor develops a favourable attitude. This may happen for one of several reasons: no recall of message, contentment with present product, the message not believed, or no differential advantage shown.

Below are selected techniques for monitoring or obtaining feedback, and several of these techniques can be combined.

Pre-test/post-test Sales or attitudes are examined prior to new promotional effort, re-examined after effort; differences are then studied.

Aided recall Recall of promotional effort is based on multiple choice questions or selection of advertisements seen from a list.

Unaided recall Recall of promotional effort is based on open-ended questions. This method measures true recall but places too much emphasis on unaided memory.

Physiological test Reactions to promotional effort are measured through skin responses and eye movements.

Monadic test Single commercial or sales presentation is evaluated.

Comparison test Two or more commercials or sales presentations are evaluated at the same time.

6 Advertisers are interested in knowing what they are getting for their advertising money. Thus, they test the proposed advertisements with a pre-test and measure actual results with a post-test.

In the past, pre-testing of advertising messages was mainly handled by advertising agencies. But increasingly advertisers are taking a more active role in the pre-testing process. There may be pre-testing either before an advertisement has been designed and executed, after it is ready for public distribution, or at both points.

During pre-testing, there is often research on three vital questions.

(a) Do consumers feel that the advertisement communicates something about the product?

(b) Does the message have an exclusive appeal that differentiates the product from competitors?

(c) Is the advertisement believable?

Although advertisers spend money primarily on pre-testing, they also post-test their promotional campaigns. There are at least three distinct reasons for measuring advertising results:

(a) to produce more effective advertising;

(b) to prove to management that a higher advertisement budget will benefit the company;

(c) to determine what level of advertising expenditure is most promising.

It is a striking fact that businesses spend billions of pounds on advertising without any clear sense of the 'pay-off' from this investment. Often there is no measurement or detailed evaluation. Even when a ratio between advertising and sales can be established, it is still of dubious value, since the relationship between advertising and sales is so unclear.

Most research focuses on communication effort rather than sales effort. The short-term effect of advertising on sales is, no doubt, tiny and unimportant, whereas, in the long run, its effect on brands and companies may be of great importance. For this reason advertisers are particularly concerned with their impact on consumer awareness and attitudes.

The main goals of advertising are to capture the attention of a potential buyer and promote brand awareness. Awareness goals are a favourable or at least curious attitude towards the product, which leads to experimentation. If this is satisfactory, the consumer may stick with the product.

There are many credible yet unresolved issues in determining how to test the communications effect of advertising. Among these are:

(a) Exposure conditions — should advertising be tested under realistic conditions or under more controlled laboratory conditions?

(b) Execution — it is often expensive and time-consuming to pre-test a finished advertisement. Does pre-testing a preliminary execution produce accurate and useful data?

(c) Quality versus quantity data — quantitative data are easiest and most precise for measurement purposes, but qualitative data from in-depth interviews can provide information that short-answer questions never can.

7 The presentation of a message involves careful evaluation of the message structure, the arrangement of measured arguments from the sort of impact given in the message, the format development, the choice of words, pictures, symbols, colours and action to conceptualise the advertising theme.

There are many distinctive forms of advertising messages. Among the most common are:

(a) The sales pitch presentation — the audience is informed about a product with a sense of urgency: 'You can't afford to miss this opportunity.'

(b) The demonstration presentation — the main goal is to show the viewer how to use an unfamiliar product while at the same time stressing its value.

(c) The mood presentation — this focuses on creating an emotional climate in which to mention the product rather than on the attributes of the product itself. We might see a young couple out in the woods, obviously in love, quiet and contented — any one of many products come to mind.

A testimonial can be presented as any one of or any combination of these three message forms. In the Brut advertising with their highly successful range of commercials, Henry Cooper comes across as an honest, believable and sincere person. He does not seem like a hustling salesman. The mood created is pleasant, a familiar, trusted celebrity presents a product in a low key manner.

Humourous messages have become an increasingly popular way of producing a mood. Another common mood-setter is the sex-oriented message, from cosmetic to conveyor-belt advertising.

8 To establish advertising objectives, we must firstly look at the role of advertising in marketing and promotion strategies. Secondly, we must focus on the advertising objectives for a given advertising programme.

A successful advertising plan must be part of a total marketing strategy that coordinates all important marketing elements including personal selling, pricing and distribution. Clear marketing goals must be established before the specifics of an advertising campaign can be formulated. Of course, the more the company can pinpoint its objectives, the better it will be for advertising purposes.

It is important to consider the advertising opportunity, i.e. the likelihood that the proposed campaign can generate sales increases substantial enough to pay its own costs and boost the firm's profits. An intelligent marketer will ask, 'Should we advertise?' before committing the company to an expensive campaign. Advertising opportunity varies among different industries, different products, and even different brands.

Primary advertising is often necessary when a company is the first to introduce a new product, or is opening up a new market for an established product. It may also be used if a company has a leading market share of an established product and wants to expand sales.

Selective advertising is aimed at promoting awareness and sales of the brand or service. Six factors shape the opportunity for selective advertising:

(a) The product offering meets some important consumer need.

(b) The product is unique or highly differentiated.

(c) The product has hidden attributes that the consumer cannot evaluate simply by inspecting it.

(d) Primary demand is already expanding because of favourable market acceptance.

(e) Adequate quantities of the product are available at the end of the distribution channel.

(f) There are sufficient funds to cover the cost of the advertising campaign.

Market research has indicated that only one quarter of all industrial advertisers set any basic objectives for their promotional work. And even when objectives were set, they were usually vague and somewhat superficial. Nevertheless, it is considered essential for the success of an advertising campaign that clear goals be mapped out.

For an advertising objective to be meaningful, it should demonstrate the following qualities:

(a) It must be precise.
(b) It must be communication-oriented.
(c) It must be related to sales and profit goals.

The general philosophy that advertising should focus on clear and measurable communication objectives has become known as DAGMAR (defining advertising goals, measuring advertising results). It was pioneered by Colley in 1961. At that time he wrote, 'Advertising succeeds or fails depending on how well it communicates the desired information and attitudes to the right people, at the right time, at the right cost.'

9 Once the advertising budget has been set, it must be allocated. Allocating the budget requires:

(a) the timing of advertising expenditures;
(b) the advertising strategies to fulfil objectives; and
(c) deciding on the media to be used to deliver the message.

Author's note: as items (b) and (c) have already been fully covered in other answers, only item (a) will be dealt with here.

Seasonality
An important issue in timing advertising expenditures is seasonality in product category sales. Most products have some seasonality based either on variations in consumption, or special events. The advertiser must decide whether advertising should precede or coincide with seasonal sales. For example, many

clothing manufacturers begin advertising their lines before the buying season. On the other hand, gift advertising tends to occur during the buying season.

Another decision is the level of advertising during the heaviest buying period. If 30% of camera sales occur in the pre-Christmas period, should camera advertisers devote 30% of their budget to this time period? Gearing the seasonal advertising expenditures to the level of purchasing activity is reasonable. But the danger is that heavy expenditure at one time of year may mean low advertising for the rest of the year at decreased levels of brand awareness.

Continuity versus pulsing

Another aspect of timing is whether advertisers should spend most of the budget in a few large bursts at various times of the year (pulsing) or choose a steady level of expenditures of the year (continuity). For example, if a strategy calls for 100 30-second spot commercials on television over one year, should about nine be run during a one-week period every month (pulsing) or should the advertisement be run twice a week over the whole year (continuity)? Many advertisers feel that pulsing has a greater effect on the consumer, since increased learning occurs when information is presented in concentrated segments. Others feel that the brand should be consistently advertised to ensure brand awareness and maintain a reminder effect through continous exposure.

One authority believes that continuity should win out over pulsing under the following conditions:

(a) when the objective is to maintain brand awareness;
(b) when the product is purchased frequently; and
(c) when the consumer is likely to forget the brand in the absence of some stimulus.

10 The role of advertising in the industrial promotional mix is very different from its role in the consumer promotional mix. Industrial advertising does not sell the product *per se*, but paves the way for the salesman. Advertising is designed to ensure that the industrial buyer is aware of the company and its products so that the subsequent visit by a salesman is more likely to lead to a sale. In contrast, consumer advertising plays a prominent rather than supportive role in the promotional mix. It is designed to influence the consumer to try the product.

Industrial advertising tends to support personal selling in the following ways. The importance of advertising in laying a foundation for a salesman's call is shown by the difficulty the industrial salesman has in making a first sales call without the benefit of a campaign.

Several studies have suggested that industrial advertising is cost-effective in increasing the likelihood of a sale. One large-scale research study found that when an industrial buyer is exposed to the advertising campaign before a sales call, sales increase by almost 30%.

Advertising is also a means of reducing the cost of a sales call — by increasing the chances that a prospect will receive a salesman and by decreasing the time required to make the sales presentation.

Advertising is a less important part of the promotional mix in industrial marketing for a number of reasons. The fact that personal selling is dominant in industrial communication means that advertising is less influential. One research study found that the most important influence on industrial buyers came from other executives in the company. The second most important influence was direct contact by the industrial salesman. Next came colleagues in other companies, trade shows, and promotional materials mailed by industrial sellers. Advertising was the least important item mentioned as influencing industrial buyers. Studies support the fact that industrial advertising is not designed so much to influence purchases as to create product and company awareness.

The lesser role of advertising in industrial as compared to consumer companies is demonstrated by the fact that only 10% of industrial marketers have a systematic plan to evaluate their advertising. One industrial advertiser says that despite the money spent on industrial advertising, few companies really consider it an integral part of their marketing and selling effort.

Index

Page numbers in **bold** type refer to the introductory sections of each chapter; those in roman type are to questions and those in *italics* are to answers.